THE KNITTED HOME

THE KNITTED HOME

CREATING CONTEMPORARY KNITS FOR INTERIORS

RUTH CROSS

with photography
by Ben Anders

jacqui
small

First published in 2013 by Jacqui Small LLP
an imprint of Aurum Press Ltd
7 Greenland Street
London NW1 0ND

ISBN 978 1 906417 72 7

A catalogue record for this book is available from the British Library.

2015 2014 2013
10 9 8 7 6 5 4 3 2 1

Printed in China

PUBLISHER Jacqui Small
EDITORIAL MANAGER Kerenza Swift
PROJECT EDITOR Sian Parkhouse
ART DIRECTION & DESIGN Sarah Rock
PRODUCTION Peter Colley

CONTENTS

introduction

In a world of shiny surfaces, flat pack furniture, clean lines and wanting everything done yesterday, the craft of hand knitting holds a very special place. Gaining ever more nostalgia as it's passed through the generations, knit remains as strong as ever – a method full of history and yet surprisingly relevant to the contemporary world that has developed alongside it.

Everyone has their own reasons for knitting, but the most unexpected is also one of the most attractive – it takes time. The quietly meditative process of building something with your own hands is a reason in itself to learn, let alone the beautiful things you can create and be truly proud of.

Every hand-knitted piece is made with care, warmth and character, which then radiates from the finished piece in a way so rarely found but so carefully cherished elsewhere in life. Hand knits bring soul to a space.

By combining this craft with clever and considered design, hand knitting will provide both the perfect foil and the perfect complement to contemporary life. I hope you find this book intriguing, challenging, satisfying and enjoyable and I wish you a warm welcome to *The Knitted Home*.

Ruth Cross

my inspiration

The Knitted Home brings together my love of interiors and work as a hand-knit designer. I was taught to knit aged 21 on a pair of chopsticks while on work placement in New York, left to get on with it and through trial and error made the rest up. It wasn't until I started working with other knitters that I realized everyone does it differently, but as each of us is individually taught we all assume we do it the same way.

Before learning myself I thought of hand knitting as a waste of time that could only create something old-fashioned or kitsch – I couldn't have been more wrong. As a craft it is incredibly undeveloped and yet its capabilities are endless. This, combined with an extremely personal and satisfying process that anyone can try, makes knit totally fascinating.

One of my main aims for *The Knitted Home* is to explain how knit works as a structure and to encourage experimentation around this. Although I've now learnt how to write a pattern, I've never actually followed one – I find them too definite in their instruction, leaving little room or allowance for an individual's taste and needs. The patterns I've included in *The Knitted Home* are intended to be adaptable; rather than creating a perfect copy of the example, I hope you'll be inspired to create something unique, something that is perfect for you and your home.

The role of individual design and creativity is extremely important to me. With hand knitting you invest so much time and care in each piece, it is important that it actually works with and complements your home. Ideally I hope to inspire you to create something that stands up as a piece of design in its own right, which you love all the more for it. My mantra is for hand-knitted designs to look handmade, not home-made.

To develop my own designs I find inspiration in all kinds of surprising places, absorbing anything I find interesting, from plants to architecture to music and food and just about anything in between. It doesn't matter what it is, as long as you like it. Half the skill of design is the ability to really look at things and analyse why you like what you like – is it the shape, a detail, colour or texture or something else entirely? You can then bring these elements to your creations, making them richer and more successful. By bringing together inspiration with your own sketches and design ideas you'll be able to visualize your different options before you start – dramatically increasing your chance of making something you love when it's finished! Eventually you'll see a pattern develop within your work and then you'll have found your own style.

So, all in all, after years of hand knitting everything under the sun, my hope is that *The Knitted Home* helps break the myth of the 'right' way to knit, and that it opens the door to some exciting and contemporary development of this ancient craft. Don't listen to anyone who tells you what to do, just have a go and have fun doing whatever works for you.

Happy knitting!

To get started you need to find some needles and yarn. Needles come in a whole range of sizes but to start with pick some that aren't too fiddly or too big to handle. I learnt on 6mm (no 4) which is good and remains my favourite today. What you prefer your needles to be made from is something you'll find out for yourself when you've tried a few. I like metal ones with quite short tapered points (I find long tapers will make your knitting tighter and less easy to play with), but there are also wood and plastic ones available.

BASIC KNITTING

For your first yarn try to pick something chunky and smooth in a light colour, which will make your knitting really easy to control. (Steer away from the sparkly hairy novelty yarns.) On balls of yarn there is a specified needle size written on the packing. Don't worry too much about this – it's an indication only. Charity shops are good places to pick up needles and yarns without spending a fortune. Then, when you've worked out what you like, find your local wool shop for more specific requirements – they will also provide a wealth of knowledge if you need advice and may even run a 'stitch and bitch' knitting group.

Using the instructions on pages 130–31 master the art of casting on, then try knitting and purling whole rows. You need about 20 stitches to give yourself a good-sized piece to practise on. Too few stitches and you'll have nothing to hold; too many and you'll be swamped. The instructions I've given are how I personally knit and purl. Everyone does it slightly differently, but I find this method allows me to play around with the stitches themselves more easily. If you knit differently then the simpler patterns in this book will work just fine, but for the more textural ones you will need to follow my method for a good result.

stripy lavender bags

Endless combinations of knit and purl rows exist (see the next pages for a taster), but if you're not sure where to start then don't worry – you can dip your toe into the world of knitting with this simple project and soon enough you'll have created your first ever knit.

What you need
- 6mm (no 4) needles
- a ball of Debbie Bliss Rialto Chunky
- cotton fabric for lining
- dried lavender

What you do
Knit two to make the front and the back
Cast on 18st

Rows 1 and 2 purl
Row 3 knit
Rows 4 and 5 purl
Rows 6–9 repeat Rows 2–5
Row 10 knit
Row 11 purl
Rows 12–14 knit
Row 15 purl
Row 16 knit
Row 17 purl
Rows 18–25 repeat Rows 2–9
Row 26 cast off knitwise

Sew up 3 of the sides (see page 139). Cut your lining fabric into 2 squares 2cm larger than the bag. Sew these together on 3 sides, turn through and fill with lavender. Sew up the final side and put this into your knitted bag, sew up the fourth side and sew on a loop of yarn.

Simple stripes

When you've got the hang of knitting and purling a whole row then you can start to play around. By changing the order of your knit and purl rows you will be able to create a whole range of stripes. If you simply alternate between knit and purl you'll get a flat jersey fabric – any other combination will instantly add stripes. When you are playing with the texture like this it's important to remember that fabric is double-sided. Sometimes what you originally intend as the back looks better than the front so always remember to check – you may need to turn the whole piece over.

This collection of lavender bags was made from squares of the stripes we came up with, so cast on a few stitches, try a few rows and see how you get on . . .

super easy bedthrow/blanket/scarf

This simple pattern uses big wool and needles to create a very chic effect – there are three widths depending on whether you want a scarf, a blanket or a full bedthrow. Which version and colour you go for is entirely up to you.

What you need

- 10mm (no 000) needles
- Rowan Big Wool (*we used colour 001*) Scarf requires approximately 4 balls. Blanket requires approximately 15 balls. Bedspread requires approximately 40 balls.

What you do

Cast on 21st for a scarf, 78st for a blanket or 208st for a bedthrow This pattern uses slipped stitches (or sl) at the beginning of every row to give a neat raw edge (see page 134)

Row 1 purl
Row 2 sl1 wyif, purl to end
Row 3 sl1 wyib, knit to end
Rows 4 – 9 repeat Rows 2–3
Rows 10 – 49 sl1 wyib, knit every row
Row 50 sl1 wyib, knit to last st, p1
Row 51 sl1 wyif, purl to last st, k1
Row 52 sl1 wyib, knit to last st, p1
Row 53 sl1 wyib, knit to end
Row 54 sl1 wyif, purl to end
Row 55 sl1 wyib, knit to end
Rows 56 – 91 repeat Rows 50 – 55

Row 92 sl1 wyib, knit to last st, p1
Row 93 sl1 wyif, purl to last st, k1
Row 94 sl1 wyib, knit to last st, p1
Row 95 sl1 wyif, purl to last st, k1
Row 96 sl1 wyib, knit to last st, p1
Row 97 sl1 wyib, knit to end
Row 98 sl1 wyif, purl to end
Row 99 sl1 wyib, knit to end
Row 100 sl1 wyif, purl to end
Row 101 sl1 wyib, knit to end
Rows 102 – 141 repeat Rows 92 – 101
Rows 142 – 146 repeat Rows 92 – 96
Rows 147 – 164 odd rows: sl1 wyib, knit; even rows: sl1 wyif, purl
Rows 165 – 183 odd rows: sl1 wyif, purl to last st, k1; even rows: sl 1 wyib, knit to last st, p1
Rows 184 – 201 odd rows: sl1 wyib, knit; even rows: sl1 wyif, purl
Rows 202 – 256 repeat Rows 92 – 146
Rows 257 – 298 repeat Rows 53 – 55, 50 – 52
Rows 299 – 338 sl1 wyib, knit every row
Row 339 sl1 wyib, knit to end
Row 340 sl1 wyif, purl to end

Rows 341 – 346 repeat Rows 339 – 340
Row 347 cast off purlwise

Your knitting will probably measure about the following:
Scarf 20cm wide
Blanket 75cm wide
Bedthrow 200cm wide

All three should measure 200cm long.

For instructions on how to add fringing, see page 110.

KNITTING REALLY WIDE THINGS

The best way to knit really wide things is to use circular needles. Use them exactly like normal needles and then the weight isn't taken by your wrists and a huge amount of stitches aren't squashed onto your needles. It's also easier to measure your knitting as you go along. A great top tip from one of my knitters for new pairs is to dip the middle section into very hot water then pull it out straight to uncurl them – it works.

Even the simplest knit can have a striking effect on a big scale – the warmth this blanket brings to such a clean room adds an unmissable air of invitation. You can find instructions to knit the Apple-Pie Cushion on page 56.

Introducing design

Knitting is like baking – once you've mastered the basic knit and purl stitches you can start to play around with each element of the process separately. The easiest way to experiment is simply by changing the yarn. There are no limits as to what can be considered yarn – if it's bendy and in a strip then you can knit with it. It's certainly not just wool out there.

These swatches follow exactly the same instructions but use different yarns and needle sizes so you can see how dramatic the effect can be.

Exploring yarn

To experiment with different materials cast on a number of stitches then switch between yarns to see what happens. Simply tie your new yarn onto the old one at the end of a row and start using it. Don't worry about all the loose ends at the moment. If you keep the needle size and number of stitches the same it will remain a similar width. Don't be precious with this kind of thing – just try, try, try and have a look at the results. It doesn't have to be beautiful – it's just research for yourself!

When you have found a particular stripe or combination you like, make a note of how you did it then you can work out the tension (see page 138) and use it to make a pattern for a straight-sided vase (see next page).

vase covers

One of my favourite ways to show off a piece of knitting is to hold it in front of the light, which exposes the structure perfectly. Making vase covers does this brilliantly and pushes knit away from its traditional cosy image to become something truly contemporary.

My ready-made vase cover pattern

The vase cover shown left in the picture opposite uses a combination of purls and knit stitches so is a good way to start.

What you need

- 7mm (size 2) needles
- a ball of Rowan Big Wool
- a ball of Rowan British Sheep Breeds DK
- a 48cm circumference, 26.5cm high vase (try floristry suppliers online for simple glass vases)

What you do

Using 2 strands of the DK cast on 58st

Row 1 purl

Row 2 purl

Drop your strands of DK and pick up 1 strand of Big Wool

Row 3 purl

Row 4 purl

Row 5 knit

Row 6 purl

Change to 2 strands of DK

Row 7 purl

Row 8 purl

Change to 1 strand of Big Wool

Row 9 purl

Row 10 purl

Change to 1 strand of DK

Row 11 purl

Row 12 purl

Change to 1 strand of Big Wool

Row 13 purl

Row 14 purl

Change to 2 strands of DK

Row 15 purl

Row 16 purl

Rows 17–30 repeat Rows 3–16

Change to 1 strand of Big Wool

Row 31 purl

Row 32 cast off knitwise

The wide stripe's flatter, knitted side is the right side so fold wrong sides together and sew up the side. You can then pull it onto your glass vase.

Making a vase cover with your own design

When you've created a stripe you like, you can make your own bespoke vase cover as I did for the vases shown opposite and on the next pages, the result of playing around with the different yarns and stitches found elsewhere in this book.

First take your vase and measure the circumference. Multiply this by your chosen stripe's stitch tension (see page 138 to work this out). For instance a 22cm circumference vase = 22cm x 2st/cm = 44st.

To make this cling to the vase deduct 10 per cent of the stitches (so from 44st required, cast on only 40st). Follow your own knit stripe instructions until you've got a long enough piece and cast off when you want. If you use circular needles you can literally hold the piece round the vase and see how it looks as you go along. When you are ready, sew up the side seam and pull the cover onto your vase.

Something from nothing

With any luck you've been experimenting like mad and now have masses of squares of knitting around the place. These are perfect to make into a patchwork cushion (or if you've been really productive you could try a blanket!). All you have to do is arrange all your pieces into a pattern you like and sew them up!

IT'S ALL IN THE FINISHING . . . THE ART OF SEWING, WASHING AND STEAMING

When you've got the hang of knitting you'll soon need to do some finishing. Finishing is everything you need to do when you've knitted the pieces required and getting it right makes all the difference. There must be a million ways to go about this but there are instructions as to what we do on page 140. If you follow these it should end up looking lovely!

patchwork cushion

This cushion is constructed using all the bits and pieces left over from many of the other projects in the book. Each panel is different and you can see from the image which goes where – obviously you can see what you have around and substitute what you have available for anything we have used. If you have any trial pieces that are the right size you can always use these up, too. (Some of the techniques used in these panels are covered later in the book so you might want to come back to this if you're not confident enough just yet.)

What you need
- yarn and needles as indicated
- a 50cm-square cushion pad
- 3 large buttons

What you do

Piece 1 (bottom left)
Using dark brown (shade 10) Patons Wool Blend Aran and 4.5mm (no 7) needles cast on 19st

Row 1 purl

Row 2 purl

Row 3 knit

Repeat Rows 2 & 3 until you have a piece about 10 cm wide x 30cm long. On the next purl row cast off knitwise

Piece 2 (top right)
Using grey (shade 92) Patons Merino DK and 4mm (no 8) needles cast on 57st. See page 130 for instructions on KB and PB.

Rows 1and 2 purl

Row 3 k1 KB x 31, k2

Row 4 p1 PB x 31, p2

Continue repeating Rows 3 and 4 until your piece is about 20cm wide x 20cm long

Cast off knitwise

Piece 3 (bottom second from right)
Using cream Debbie Bliss Rialto Chunky and 6.5mm (no 3) needles cast on 15st

Rows 1–63 purl

Cast off purlwise

This piece should measure about 10cm wide x 30cm long

Piece 4 (bottom right)
Using blue Debbie Bliss Rialto Chunky and 6.5mm (no 3) needles cast on 15st

Row 1 purl

Row 2 purl

Row 3 knit

Repeat Rows 2 and 3 until you have a piece about 10cm wide x 30cm long. On the next purl row cast off knitwise

Piece 5 (top left)

Using Rowan British Sheep Breeds DK undyed and 4mm (no 8) needles cast on 44st

Row 1 (k2 p2) repeat x 11

Row 2 p1 (k2 p2) x 10 k2 p1

Repeat Rows 1 and 2 until your piece is about 20cm wide x 30cm long. Cast off knitwise.

Piece 6 (bottom centre)

Using marled dark blue Patons Wool Blend Aran and 4.5mm (no 7) needles cast on 38st

Every row purl – continue until your piece is about 20 x 20cm when pulled slightly.

Pieces 7 and 8 (centre)

Using black/white Rowan Big Wool (one piece in each colour) and 7mm (no 2) needles cast on 13st

Row 1 knit

Row 2 purl

Rows 3–16 repeat Rows 1 and 2

Cast off knitwise

Each piece should measure about 10 x 10cm

When you've made all the pieces arrange them in the right order and sew them together. You can then either use the following cushion back pattern or simply sew a fabric back on – it's entirely up to you.

Back underlap

Using grey Debbie Bliss Rialto Chunky cast on 54st

Row 1 purl

Row 2 sl1 wyif, purl to end

Row 3 sl1 wyib, knit to end

Rows 4–101 repeat Rows 2 and 3

Row 102 Cast off knitwise

This piece should measure about 36cm wide x 48cm high

Back overlap

Using grey Debbie Bliss Rialto Chunky cast on 36st

Row 1 purl

Row 2 sl1 wyif, purl to end

Row 3 sl1 wyib, knit to end

Rows 4–101 repeat Rows 2 and 3 *

*On Row 21, Row 51 and Row 81 make a 6st buttonhole 3st in from the edge (see page 138)

Row 102 cast off knitwise

This piece should measure about 24cm wide x 48cm high

To sew up see page 139. Sew buttons to underlap, aligning with buttonholes.

For the pattern for the patchwork blanket (right) see pages 74–76.

The lovely thing about knit is that, in its most basic form, it is really simple to do, yet it is easily altered to create endless new designs. But by actually playing with the structure of knit a whole new world opens and allows us to create truly exceptional work – nowhere is this more obvious than with the wonderful textures possible. Hand knitting is the only method of making textiles that is so controllable in this way, and that's why we love it. However, like everything where there are no limits, it can be a bit daunting, so I'm going to explain it little by little!

CREATING TEXTURE

So far all our stripes have been horizontal with whole rows of purl or knit. By using knit and purl in the same row we can create clever patterns – the most familiar being the rib commonly used on cuffs.

A basic rib that will get you started is as follows: cast on a multiple of 4 stitches + 2. Row 1 (k2 p2) repeat to last 2 stitches, k2. Row 2 (p2 k2) repeat to last 2 stitches, p2.

Try altering your yarn and needle size to understand how ribs behave, then try altering the number of purl and knit stitches. Clever ribs can be really impressive and are often elastic enough to be used to wrap around shapes without any need to change the number of stitches.

ribbed fruit bowl cover

Ribs in their simplest form can be very effective. Just look at how they work with these chunky wooden fruit bowls, transforming them with a surprising new look.

What you need

- 7mm (no 2) needles
- a wooden bowl
- a chunky yarn (*we used Rowan Felted Tweed Chunky in colour 282 blue and 283 grey*)

What you do

First measure the widest circumference of your bowl and allow 1st per 1cm. Cast on this many stitches and start with a rib of 2 purls then 2 knits. If your total number of stitches isn't divisible by 4 then just knit/purl what you can for the last repeat. When you do the next row just follow what you have in the row below and your rib will work out fine.

To work out how many rows you need for this section, measure where you want the cover to start on the base of the bowl to where the widest part is. (Start just in from where the side starts – if your bowl is fairly flat like ours most of the base will not be covered.) Work as many rows as you need to get this length. At this point change to a 3 purls, 3 knits rib (if your row isn't divisible by 6 then do as for the first rib and cut the last repeat short). Work as many rows as you need to reach the top of the bowl, then cast off tightly.

Sew up the side seam and pull the cover over the bowl top first. The rib will spring in to wrap around the bowl's base but to make sure it stays put we used a long piece of the yarn and went through each stitch of the cast on and pulled it closed like a drawstring to make the cover really snug. The firm cast-off edge should be slightly smaller than the bowl's lip and will hold on to this edge – if it is a bit baggy and looks like it might slip down just sew a similar drawstring thread around the top too.

These are really quick and easy and there isn't any limit to what shape they can be made for – just use the 2 x 2 rib where you need a tighter spring and a larger rib for a more relaxed fabric.

combining knits and purls for texture

Try combining knits and purls in any order to discover patterns for yourself. As you can see from the table runner on pages 40–43, knit (essentially a grid) lends itself easily to checks and stripes, but if you can find diagonal patterns they can be even more effective.

Cast on a good few stitches and get started, changing and adapting your ideas as you go (sometimes sketching ideas before can help). However, be careful to give each possible pattern enough stitches and rows to see how it works on a big scale – sometimes patterns just need a bit of consistent repetition to reveal themselves.

Three simple knit/purl stitch patterns to try

Simply repeat the stitches indicated within (brackets) as instructed

Fake basket weave
Cast on a multiple of 6st + 1
Row 1 (p1 k2) to last st, p1
Row 2 k1 (p2 k1) to end
Row 3 (p4 k2) to last st, p1
Row 4 k1 (p2 k4) to end
Rows 5 and 6 repeats Rows 1 and 2
Row 7 p1 (k2 p4) to end
Row 8 (k4 p2) to last st, k1
Repeat Rows 1–8

Mistake stitch rib
Cast on a multiple of 4st + 3
There is only one instruction to this stitch:
(k2 p2) to last 3 st, k2 p1 – do every row like this!

Texture diamonds
Cast on a multiple of 8st + 3
Row 1 k1 (p2 k5 p1) to last 2 st, p1 k1
Row 2 p2 (k2 p3 k2 p1) to last st, p1
Row 3 k3 (p2 k1 p2 k3) to end
Row 4 p4 (k3 p5) to last 7 st, k3 p4
Row 5 k4 p3 (k5 p3) to last 4 st, k4
Row 6 p3 (k2 p1 k2 p3) to end
Row 7 k2 (p2 k3 p2 k1) k1
Row 8 p1 (k2 p5 k1) to last 2 st, k1 p1
Repeat Rows 1–8

adaptable table runner

Combining knits and purls is a simple way to build up a larger-scale pattern and by introducing simple details, as this runner has, we can create something easily yet remarkably chic looking.

HOW TO USE REPEATS USING THIS RUNNER AS AN EXAMPLE

Measure how big you would like your piece to be. Using the repeat measurements, you can work out what you need as follows:

Take the width of knitting you would like, subtract the width of the additional edge stitches, then divide the rest by the width of one repeat. This will tell you how many repeats and stitches you need. However, this sum almost never works out exactly, so depending on the look you want you must decide if you want to make it a bit bigger/smaller by rounding up/down the amount you cast on.

Each repeat (using the yarn and needles specified) is 22st/approx 11.5cm wide x 30 rows/approx 11cm long. Onto this you need to add 9 additional stitches for the edges of the width (+3cm) and 7 rows (+2cm) for the start and end of the piece. Of course if you like the pattern but want it in a different yarn you can just do a few repeats as a stitch sample and use the measurements you take from it.

What you need

- 4mm (no 8) needles
- Debbie Bliss Amalfi (*we used 10 balls of colour 011*)
- 2mm-wide ribbon, ideally viscose (*we used 86m not including the fringing*)

How much you need of these depends on the size of the piece you make and the ribbon is optional – you could use a contrasting colour yarn or ignore this detail completely.

What you do

Cast on (using the ribbon) a multiple of 22st + 9. (*We cast on 75st or 3 repeats*)

The 22st repeat section is shown in [square brackets], the pattern repeats within this are shown in (round brackets).

Row 1 purl

Change to the Amalfi yarn

Row 2 sl1 wyif, p1 [p12 k3 p7] x3, p7

Row 3 sl1 wyib, k1 [(k1 p1) x6, p3 (p1 k1) x 3 p1] x 3, k1 (p1 K1) x2, k2

Row 4 as Row 2

Row 5 sl1 wyib, k1 [(p1 k1) x 6, p3 (k1 p1) x 3, k1] x 3, p1 (k1 p1) x 2, k2

Row 6 as Row 2

Row 7 as Row 3

Row 8 as Row 2

Row 9 sl1 wyib, k1 [(p1 k1) x 2, p1 k7 p3 k7] x 3, (p1 k1) x 2, p1 k2

Row 10 as Row 2

Row 11 sl1 wyib, k1 [(k1 p1) x 2, k8 p3 k7]) x 3, (k1 p1) x 2, k3

Row 12 as Row 8

Row 13 as Row 9

Row 14 as Row 8

Row 15 as Row 11

Row 16 as Row 2

Row 17 sl1 wyib, k1, purl to last 2st k2

Row 18 sl1 wyif, p1, knit to last 2st p2

Row 19 as Row 17

Row 20 as Row 8

continued on next page

Row 21 as Row 11
Row 22 as Row 2
Row 23 as Row 9
Row 24 as Row 2
Row 25 as Row 11
Row 26 as Row 2
Row 27 as Row 9
Row 28 as Row 2
Row 29 as Row 3
Row 30 as Row 2
Row 31 as Row 5
Change to ribbon
Row 32 as Row 2
Row 33 as Row 3
Change to Amalfi yarn
Row 34 as Row 2
Row 35 as Row 5
Row 36 as Row 2
Row 37 as Row 3

Rows 8–37 are one repeat lengthways. Do as many of these as you need. Then to finish repeat Rows 8–33 only and on your next row cast off using the ribbon. We did 23 repeats overall lengthways and the runner measures just over 265cm long x 35cm wide.

We then used the same ribbon to fringe the ends – see the embellishment section (page 110) for help with this.

Everything so far in this book should be taken as a guide – don't think for a second there are actually any set rules to knitting (beyond making sure the basic structure holds together). By now you'll understand that knitting is just a chain that links horizontally and vertically. As long as each stitch of the chain is secure you can start to challenge the basics. The most interesting ideas will come out of not being precious about your experimenting and always asking yourself 'what happens if . . . ?' Just remember that almost anything in repetition will look good!

MANIPULATING STITCHES

I first started to 'manipulate' stitches when I realized how much else there was to explore within the structure. Taking inspiration from an interesting texture, I start to work out how to knit something similar. If it's an uneven look you want, try to be messy – change needles or yarns randomly or work the same stitches several times to create textural bumps. You can intentionally start ladders, sew bits together or add knitting to other things by hooking them onto your needle like stitches. On the other hand you can be super precise and develop a really clean, sleek finished cloth. To get started don't worry too much about what it looks like. Just dive in – who knows what you will discover?

introducing new techniques

Below are a few new things to try and some simple patterns for each technique, shown in the samples opposite (clockwise from top left) and in some of the cushions on the following page.

Basket Stitches

One of my favourite techniques is the basket stitch. I'm sure it has many other names but this is what I know it as. See page 130 for instructions on KB and PB.

Cast on an odd number of stitches, knit a row or two then repeat these two rows

Row 1 (KB) to last stitch k1
Row 2 (PB) to last stitch p1

Extra long stitches

To create an open section in your knitting try wrapping the yarn around the needle more than once before you pull through the new stitch. The extra wrap will stay on your needle until the next row when you work it as normal and the long stitch will unwrap itself. You can wrap as many times as you like, as often as you like – there are limitless combinations but here is a simple one to try first:

Cast on any number of stitches
Row 1 purl
Row 2 double length purl
(to get double length wrap the yarn round twice before pulling the purl stitch through)
Repeat these rows
(used in cushion far left, page 48)

Lace holes

Lace holes are created by doing a combination of togs and yos (see pages 135 and 136). If you do these actions next to each other you make a neat hole. If you do some normal stitches between the actions you'll get the illusion of whole sections of stitches moving diagonally.

A basic example is as follows:
Cast on a multiple of 12st + 1
Row 1 knit
Row 2 p1 (p2 tog p9 yo k1)
Repeat Rows 1 and 2
(A similar pattern is used in the far right cushion on page 49. Once you get the idea, try a variation of this and use a different number of plain stitches between the yos and togs. Have some fun with it.)

Cables

Whole books are written about this simple yet effective technique, known for looking really impressive. See page 137 for the theory of knitting cables.

A simple cable to try is as follows:
Cast on a multiple of 4st + 2
Row 1 knit
Row 2 purl
Row 3 k1 (sl2 st to cn and hold in front, k2, k2 from cn) to last stitch k1
Row 4 purl
Repeat Rows 1 and 4
(A similar cable pattern is used in the central cushion on pages 48–49.)

When you have a sample of knitting you like see page 138 for instructions on how to work out your tension. Then you can work out how to knit something of a particular size.

Designing patterns

Patterns are created by altering and combining different stitches, yarns or colours. You can of course do all of these at once, but to keep it chic make it as simple as possible. I try to stick to the rule that three elements of a design is enough. If there are more than this it can look confusing as each element loses some of its strength. A single design element is anything from a novelty yarn to a stripe to a pretty trim – anything that is a designed feature rather than just the absolute basic requirements for the design.

These cushions are all the same tones and size – the only difference is the stitch pattern, which counts as one element of design. As you can see, texture is so important as it makes such a difference, but in a clever way, and the group works beautifully as a set.

From left the cushions show extra long stitch (see page 47), zig-zag stitch (see pages 50–51 for full pattern), cables (for an example see page 47), X pattern (see pages 52–55 for full pattern) and lace holes (for an example see page 47).

DESIGNING PATTERNS **49**

zig-zag cushion

Also shown on page 48, this zig-zag patterned cushion cover uses a simple stitch combination that creates the illusion of a geometric weave rather than a knit. By playing with the structure to make designs this clean looking, we allow knit to hold its own in interiors as contemporary as these.

What you need

- 6mm (no 4) needles
- Debbie Bliss Rialto Chunky (*we used 6 balls of colour 002*)
- a 38cm-square cushion pad
- a button

What you do

The front

This measures about 36 x 36cm. See page 130 for instructions on KB and PB.

Cast on 68st

Rows 1-2 purl

Row 3 sl1 wyib k1 (KB k1) x 22

Row 4 sl1 wyif, purl to end

Row 5 sl1 wyib k2 (KB k1) x 21, k2

Row 6 sl1 wyif, purl to end

Row 7 sl1 wyib (KB k1) x22, k1

Row 8 sl1 wyif P1 (p1 PB)x 21, p3

Row 9 sl1 wyib, knit to end

Row 10 sl1 wyif PB (p1 PB) x21, p2

Row 11 as Row 9

Row 12 sl1 wyif (p1 PB) x 22, p1

Row 13 as Row 9

Row 14 as Row 8

Row 15 as Row 7

Row 16 as Row 4

Rows 3–16 is one repeat. Do 3 more full repeats. Then repeat Rows 3–12. Cast off purlwise

The back underlap

This measures about 30cm wide x 36cm high

Cast on 46st

Row 1 purl

Row 2 sl1 wyif, purl to end

Row 3 sl1 wyib, knit to end

Rows 4–71 repeat Rows 2 and3

Cast off knitwise

The back overlap with buttonhole

This measures about 18cm wide x 36cm high

Cast on 28st

Row 1 purl

Row 2 sl1 wyif, purl to end

Row 3 sl1 wyib, knit to end

Rows 4–71 repeat Rows 2 and 3 *

*on Row 35 knit 3 stitches then make a 6st buttonhole (see page 138). Cast off knitwise

To sew up see page 139. Sew button to underlap, aligning with buttonhole.

x pattern cushion

This is the sister pattern for the zig-zag cushion (see previous pages) but has a complicated bit in the middle, so master the zig-zag first. The technique for this is venturing into the realm of what I think of as 'purist' knitting, the re-thinking of how we expect things to work in order to make something beautiful, new and perfect – even if it does look deceptively simple when finished. Go on, challenge yourself!

What you need
- 6mm (no 4) needles
- Debbie Bliss Rialto Chunky (*we used 6 balls of colour 002*)
- a 38cm-square cushion pad
- a button

What you do
The front
This should measure 36 x 36cm – always make cushion covers a bit small or they look baggy. See page 130 for instructions on KB and PB. Cast on 67st

Row 1 purl

Row 2 purl

Row 3 sl1 wyib k1 (k1 KB) x 10, k2 k33

Row 4 sl 1 wyif p1 (p1 PB) x 10, p2 p33

Row 5 sl1 wyib (KB k1) x 11, k33

Row 6 sl1 wyif (PB p1) x 11, p33

Row 7 sl1 wyib (k1 KB) x 11, k33

Row 8 sl1 wyif (p1 PB) x 11, p33

Rows 9–38 repeat Rows 3–8

Row 39 slip all the stitches onto the other needle and cut the yarn leaving a long end for sewing. Take your yarn again and start from this end. Because you have slipped the stitches instead of knitting them they may be hanging on the needle the wrong way around – you may have to turn each stitch before you work it as otherwise it may end up with a twist in it which won't look so good.

Row 40 sl1 wyif p33 (PB p1) x 11

Row 41 sl1 wyib k33 (KB k1) x 11

Row 42 sl1 wyif p33 (p1 PB) x 10, p3

Row 43 sl1 wyib k33 (k1 KB) x 10, k3

Row 44 sl1 wyif p32 (PB p1) x 11, p1

Row 45 sl1 wyib k32 (KB k1) x 11, k1

Rows 46–75 repeat Rows 40–45

Cast off purlwise

For the back see the Zig-zag cushion pattern on page 50.

To sew up see page 139. Sew button to underlap, aligning with buttonhole.

The X cushion is shown here with the patchwork blanket (see pages 74–77) and patchwork cushion (see pages 30–32), showing how different styles can contrast in an interesting way. If you like the clean lines of the zig-zag and X cushions and want a patchwork blanket to match you could create one that incorporates the cushion fronts as panels within the patchwork.

apple-pie cushion

I call this the apple-pie cable as it reminds me of latticed pastry on top of an apple pie. It's also a very cosy, homely and warm cable, perfect for duvet days and winter nights.

What you need
- 6.5mm (no 3) needles
- Debbie Bliss Rialto Chunky (*we used 12 balls of colour 003*)
- a 50cm-square cushion pad
- 3 lovely big buttons
- a cable needle (cn)

What you do
The front
This should measure about 48 x 48cm – always make cushion covers small or they look baggy. Cast on 118st

Row 1 purl

Row 2 purl

Row 3 sl1 wyib k2 sl2 wyib k108 sl2 wyib k3

Row 4 sl1 wyif p2 sl2 wyif p108 sl2 wyif p3

Row 5 sl1 wyib (sl2 to cn, hold in back, k1, k2 from cn, sl1 to cn, hold in front, k2 k1 from cn; this is called Bird Cable) k4 (sl4 to cn, hold in front k4,k4 from cn; this is called 8st Cable Front) x 6 (sl4 to cn and hold in back, k4, k4 from cn (this is called 8st Cable Back) x 6 k4 (Bird Cable) k1

Row 6 sl1 wyif purl to end

Row 7 as Row 3

Row 8 as Row 4

Row 9 sl1 wyib (Bird Cable) k104 (Bird Cable) k1

Row 10 as Row 6

Row 11 sl1 wyib k2 sl2 wyib k2 (8st Cable Back) x6, k8 (8st Cable Front) x6, k2 sl2 wyib k3

Row 12 as Row 4

Row 13 as Row 9

Row 14 as Row 6

Rows 15 – 122 repeat Rows 3 – 14

Rows 123 – 127 repeat Rows 3 – 7

Cast off knitwise

For the back instructions see the Patchwork cushion cover pattern on page 32.

To sew up see page 139. Sew buttons to underlap, aligning with buttonholes.

Here on the side of the cushion you can see the structure of the apple-pie cable alongside the bird cable edging. This adds subtlety and finish to what is an otherwise simple design.

Finding good buttons . . .

 . . . is much harder than you might expect, so pick them up when you find them. We especially love big vintage buttons and toggles, which make the back of cushions just as pretty as the front.

geometric cable throw

This is 190cm long and not for the faint-hearted but is very rewarding when it's finished! We fringed ours randomly – follow the fringing instructions on page 110 if you'd like to do this too and allow for extra wool.

What you need

- 7mm (no 2) circular needles
- Rowan British Sheep Breeds Chunky Undyed (*we used 20 balls of colour 954*)
- a cable needle (cn)

VARIATIONS

If you like the pattern of this but don't like the chunkiness or yarn then why not decide your own yarn, needles and size. The repeat widthways is 64 stitches and then you need to add 4 stitches for the edges. Knit yourself a sample with your preferred needles and yarn and use the repeat instructions to work out how many stitches and rows you need. You could do a really fine version or a smaller version and make a cushion cover – whatever you feel like is possible. Just be cautious that open loose knitting doesn't generally look good cabled, so keep it quite tight.

What you do

Cast on 196st – you definitely need circular needles for all these stitches!

Row 1 purl

Row 2 purl

Row 3 (and all other non-cable odd rows) knit

Row 4 (and every other even row) purl

Row 5 k2 [(slip 4st to cn and hold in back, k4 k4 from cn; this is called Cable Back) x4, (sl4 to cn and hold in front, k4 k4 from cn; this is called Cable Front) x4] x 3, k2

Row 11 k2 [k4 (Cable Front) k4 (Cable Back) x2, (Cable Front) x2 k4 (Cable Back) k4] x3, k2

Row 17 as Row 5

Row 23 k2 [(Cable Back) k4 (Cable Front) k4 (Cable Back) (Cable Front) k4 (Cable Back) k4 (Cable Front)] x3, k2

Row 29 as Row 5

Row 35 k2 [(Cable Back) x2, k4 (Cable Front) k8 (Cable Back) k4 (Cable Front) x2] x3, k2

Row 41 as Row 5

Row 45 k2 [(Cable Front) x4, (Cable Back) x 4] x3, k2

Row 51 k2 [(Cable Front) x2, k4 (Cable Back) k8 (Cable Front) k4 (Cable Back) x2] x3, k2

Row 57 as Row 45

Row 63 k2 [(Cable Front) k4 (Cable Back) k4 (Cable Front) (Cable Back) k4 (Cable Front) k4 (Cable Back)] x3, k2

Row 69 as Row 45

Row 75 k2 [k4 (Cable Back) k4 (Cable Front) x2, (Cable Back) x2, k4 (Cable Front) k4] x3, k2

Row 81 as Row 45

Rows 82–321 repeat Rows 2–81

Row 322 cast off knitwise

This huge cable repeat doesn't become clear until you see it on such a big scale and the full pattern reveals itself. We added a random fringe to soften this otherwise uniform design, but you could also add a fabric back or even knit a plain one to make the throw double-sided.

Sometimes you'll want your pattern to only cover part of your knitting, or to have sections of different patterns across a piece to create more complicated designs. To work this out you just need to be methodical and then the results should be perfect – whether it's a patterned stripe on a plain background or a 'patchwork' blanket of different patterns that is actually knitted in one piece.

COMBINING PATTERNS

Decide what patterns you would like to use, knit a sample and work out your tension for each (following the instructions on page 138). If you're using cables just measure the width of your sample cable. It will make life a lot easier if you pick patterns you like that are all knitted on the same size needles with the same yarn.

You can play around with your samples to see how the patterns look together and do some sketches of what kind of layout you would like the final piece to have. Start with something of a simple shape, like a cushion or a throw, and decide the size. Then start to work out how much you'd like to cover with each pattern across the width. Think also about whether you would like some kind of detail on the edge, and include this in your working out if you do. You can then follow the instructions on pages 141–43 to work out your final full pattern.

bolster cushion

This bolster cushion is a perfect example of combining textures in one piece effectively. Using different textures but keeping the shape and yarn simple like this will create something truly striking for any style of interior.

We worked out this pattern for a bolster cushion using the method described on pages 141–42

What you need
- 5.5mm (no 5) needles
- a cable needle (cn)
- Patons Merino Wool DK (*we used 7 balls of colour 92*)
- a cushion pad about 60cm wide x 30cm high
- 2 buttons

Pattern layout

8st Cables – arrow direction indicates cable direction
NB Average row tension = 2.13r/cm – you need this to work out length

59cm

MOSS STITCH

BASKET STITCH

MOSS STITCH

25.5cm length = 64r (average r/cm=2.13)

6.35cm = **9st**

Bird Cable 2.5cm = **6st**

2 x 8st Cable 6.35cm = **16 st**

5.8cm = **15st**

2 x 8st Cable 6.35cm = **16 sts**

2 x 4st Cable = 3.8cm **8st**

6.5cm = **9st**

8st Cable 3.2cm = **8 sts**

Bird Cable = 2.5cm **6st**

2 x 8st Cable 6.35cm = **16 sts**

2 x 4st Cable = 3.8cm **8st**

Stocking Stitch = 3cm **4st**

Bird Cable = 2.cm **6st**

Total stitches = 127 + 1 extra for each end = **Cast on 129st**
Follow instructions for each row of each section for 64 rows

Stitch tensions and measurements from swatch:
Moss stitch = 1.47st/cm 2r/cm
4st cable = 1.9cm wide 2r/cm
Bird cable = 2.5cm wide 2.28r/cm

8st cable = 3.3cm wide 2r/cm
Basket stitch = 2.5st/cm 1.82r/cm
Stocking stitch = 1.33st/cm 2.5r/cm

A clever use of contrasting colour makes the bolster cushion right at home on this lemon-coloured chair, whilst the Super Easy Bedthrow seen on the previous pages (see page 16 for the pattern) complements the more organic aspects of the interior.

What you do

See page 130 for instructions on KB and PB.

Front Panel (about 58 x 28cm)
Cast on 129st (using two balls held together)
Row 1 purl
Row 2 purl
Row 3 sl1 wyib k2 sl2 wyib k32 sl2 wyib k10 (k1 p1) x4, k25 (KB) x7, k17 (k1 p1) x4, k3 sl2 wyib k3

Row 4 sl1 wyif p2 sl2 wyif p27 (PB) x7, p44 sl2 wyif p32 sl2 wyif p3
Row 5 sl1 wyib (sl2 to cn, hold in back, k1, k2 from cn, sl1 to cn, hold in front, k2, k1 from cn; this is called Bird Cable) k4 (sl2 to cn, hold in back, k2, k2 from cn; this is called 4st Cable Back) (sl2 to cn, hold in front, k2, k2 from cn; this is called 4st Cable Front) k16 (Bird Cable) k8 (p1 k1) x4, p1 (4st Cable Back) (4st Cable Front) k16 (KB) x7, k17

(p1 k1) x4, p1 (Bird Cable) k1
Row 6 sl1 wyif p31, (PB) x7, purl to end
Row 7 sl1 wyib k2 sl2 wyib k14 (sl4 to cn, hold in back, k4, k4 from cn; this is called 8st Cable Back) x2, k2 sl2 wyib k2 (sl4 to cn, hold in front, k4, k4 from cn; this is called 8st Cable Front) (k1 p1) x4, k9 (8st Cable Back) (8st Cable Front) (KB) x7, k1 (8st Cable Back) x2, (k1 p1) x4, k3 sl2 wyib k3

Row 8 as Row 4
Row 9 as Row 5
Row 10 as Row 6
Rows 11–66 repeat Rows 3–10
Row 66 cast off knitwise

**Back Underlap
(29cm wide x 28cm long)**
Cast on 44st (using 2 balls held together)
Row 1 purl
Row 2 sl1 wyif, purl to end

Row 3 sl1 wyib, knit to end
Rows 4–59 repeat Rows 2 and3
Row 60 cast off knitwise

**Back Overlap
(44cm wide x 28 cm long)**
Cast on 66st (using two balls held together)
Row 1 purl
Row 2 sl1 wyif, purl to end
Row 3 sl1 wyib, knit to end
Rows 4 – 59 repeat Rows 2 and 3*

Row 60 cast off knitwise
* On Rows 15 and 45 make a 5st buttonhole 4 sts into the row (see page 138 for how to make buttonholes)

To sew up see page 139. Sew buttons to underlap, aligning with buttonholes.

patchwork blanket

This blanket was made using yarns found throughout this book, but of course you can substitute these for whatever suits your home – totally multi-coloured and multi-textural, or shades of one colour in the same yarn for a more minimal look. The possibilities are endless.

What you do

Border pieces

There are 4 of these pieces – 2 long and 2 short. The longer ones measure 1.5m wide to start and grow to 162cm at Row 19. The shorter ones measure 100cm wide to start and grow to 116cm at row 119. Both are 16cm long overall.

Using chocolate (shade 10) Patons Wool Blend Aran and 4.5mm (no 7) needles cast on 285/190st

Row 1 purl

Row 2 purl

Row 3 sl1 wyib k2 yo, knit to last 3 sts yo k3 (287/192st)

When working the yo make sure they have twists and do not create lace holes (see page 136 for explanations of yo).

Row 4 sl1 wyif p2 yo, purl to last 3 sts yo p3 (289/194st)

Rows 5–18 as Rows 3–4 (317/222 sts)

Row 19 knit

Row 20 purl

Row 21 sl1 wyib k2 k2tog, knit to last 5 sts, k2tog k3 (315/220st)

Row 22 sl1 wyif p2 p2tog, purl to last 5 sts p2tog p3 (313/218st)

Row 23 – 36 as Rows 21 – 22 (285/190st)

Row 37 knit

Row 38 cast off knitwise

Piece 1

60cm wide x 90cm long
See page 130 for instructions on KB and PB. Using blue Debbie Bliss Rialto Chunky and 6.5mm (no 3) needles cast on 90st

Row 1 purl

Row 2 purl

Row 3 knit

Rows 4–9 as Rows 2 and 3

Row 10 p1 PB x 44 p1

Row 11 k2 KB x 43 k2

Rows 12–61 repeat Rows 2–11

Rows 62 – 169 repeat Rows 2 – 9

Row 170 cast off knitwise

Piece 2

30cm wide x 40cm long
Using beige Debbie Bliss Amalfi and 4mm (size 8) needles cast on 66st

Row 1 purl

Row 2 purl

Row 3 knit

Rows 4–11 as Rows 2 and 3

Row 12 knit

Row 13 purl

Rows 14–17 as Rows 12 and13

Rows 18–121 repeat Rows 2–17

Rows 122 cast off knitwise

Piece 3

20cm wide x 80cm long
Using black Rowan Big Wool and 10mm (no 000) needles cast on 24st (you will also need a cable needle)

Row 1 purl

Row 2 purl

Row 3 knit

Row 4 purl

Row 5 k2 (sl3 to cn, hold in back k3, k3 from cn, k1) x2, sl3 to cn, hold in front, k3, k3 from cn, k2

Row 6 purl

Row 7 knit

Rows 2–7 is one repeat – continue repeating this section until your piece is 80cm long and then cast off knitwise

Piece 4

20cm wide x 50cm long
Using marled brown (shade 14)
Patons Wool Blend Aran and
4.5mm (no 7) needles cast on 38st
Row 1 purl
Row 2 purl
Row 3 knit
Repeat Rows 2–3 until you have
a piece 50cm long and then cast
off knitwise

Piece 5

20 x 20cm
Using grey (shade 92) Patons
Merino DK and 4mm (no 8) needles
cast on 40st
Row 1 purl
Row 2 purl
Row 3 knit
Repeat Rows 2 and 3 until you have
a piece 20cm long and then cast
off knitwise

Piece 6

10cm wide x 30cm long
Using lilac Debbie Bliss Rialto
Chunky and 6.5mm (no 3) needles
cast on 15st
Rows 1–64 purl
Cast off purlwise

Piece 7

40cm wide x 90cm
Using Rowan British Sheep Breeds
undyed DK and 4mm (size 8)
needles cast on 88st
Row 1 (k2 p2) x22
Row 2 p1 (k2 p2) x21, k2 p1
Repeat Rows 1 and 2 until your
piece is 90cm long then cast off

Piece 8

40cm wide x 30cm long
Using grey (shade 92) Patons
Merino DK and 5.5mm (size 5)
needles cast on 89st using 2 balls
held together
(you will also need a cable needle)
Row 1 purl
Row 2 purl
Row 3 k9 (k1 p1) x4, k25 (KB) x7,
k17 (k1 p1) x4, k3 sl2 wyib k3
Row 4 sl1 wyif p2 sl2 wyif p27 PB
x7, purl to end
Row 5 k9 (p1 k1) x4, p1 (sl2 to cn,
hold in back, k2, k2 from cn; this is
called 4st cable back) (sl2 to cn,
hold in front, k2, k2 from cn; this is
called 4st Cable Front) k16 (KB) x7,
k17 (p1 k1) x4, p1 (sl2 to cn, hold in
back, k1, k2 from cn, sl1 to cn, hold
in front, k2, k1 from cn; this is called
Bird Cable) k1
Row 6 sl1 wyif p31 (PB) x7, purl to
end
Row 7 k1 (sl4 to cn, hold in front,
k4, k4 from cn; this is called 8st
Cable Front) (k1 p1) x4, k9 (sl4 to
cn, hold in back, k4, k4 from cn;
this is called 8st Cable Back) (8st
cable front) (KB) x7, k1 (8st Cable
Back) x2, (k1 p1) x4, k3 sl2 wyib k3
Row 8 as Row 4
Row 9 as Row 5
Row 10 as Row 6
Rows 11–66 repeat Rows 3 – 10
Row 66 cast off knitwise

Piece 9

20 x 20cm
Using grey (shade 92) Patons
Merino DK and 4mm (no 8) needles
cast on 44st
Rows 1–60 knit
Cast off knitwise

Piece 10

10 x 10cm
Using black Rowan Big Wool and
7mm (no 2) needles cast on 13st
Row 1 knit
Row 2 purl
Rows 3–16 repeat Rows 1 and 2
Cast off knitwise

Piece 11

20 x 20cm
Using burgundy Debbie Bliss
Rialto Chunky and 6.5mm (no 3)
needles cast on 30st
Rows 1–8 (k5 p5) x3
Rows 9–11 (p5 k5) x3
Rows 12–19 as Rows 1–8
Rows 20–26 as Rows 9–11
Rows 27–30 as Rows 1–8
Rows 31–35 as Rows 9–11
Rows 36–38 as Rows 1–8
Cast off purlwise

Lay the pieces out as shown and
sew everything together except the
border. Pin the ends of the border
together and sew up so you have a
rectangle. Lay your rectangle right
sides together on the front of the
blanket and overstitch through the
front layer only all the way around.
Fold the border over to the back of
the piece and sew it neatly in place.

long border

7   11   9   5

1

6   10

4   2   8

3

short border

Inserting a contrasting yarn as a vertical panel

You can also add vertical stripes into knitting by changing your yarn. The proper name for this is 'intarsia' and it is often used to create pictures on jumpers (this is the technique used to create novelty or themed jumpers, such as reindeers at Christmas). The technique is actually quite under developed, but enormously satisfying and beautiful when you've cracked it.

The basic theory is that as you work along the row instead of allocating different stitch instructions to make the sections you change yarns. Each section will need its own ball and you'll need a system to keep them in order and untangled or total chaos will take over pretty quickly! I line them up on the floor around me and make sure I alternate the way I turn the knitting at the end of each row – it seems to work. For technical instructions see page 140.

intarsia blanket

About as far from a Christmas jumper as you can get, this beautiful intarsia blanket combines yarns of subtly different shades and weights to striking contemporary effect.

What you need

- 10mm (no 000) needles
- Rowan Big Wool (*we used 5 balls of colour 001*)
- Rowan British Sheep Breeds DK Undyed (*we used 9 balls of colour 780 ecru*)

This blanket measures about 1.1m wide x 1.5m long

What you do

Cast on 114st including yarn changes as follows – see page 140 for detailed instructions on how to manage this

Big Wool (BW) cast on 18st
Two balls of DK together (2 x DK) cast on 6st
BW cast on 30st
2 x DK cast on 6st
BW cast on 30st
2 x DK cast on 6st
BW cast on 18st

Row 1 Purl entire row changing from one yarn to the next as shown in the row beneath it

Row 2 Knit entire row changing from one yarn to the next as shown in the row beneath it

Rows 3–11 repeat Rows 1 and 2

Row 12 BW k6. Take the next 2 x DK (12st early) change over to the DK and k30. Take the BW (12st late) change over to the BW and k6. Continue changing like this:

2 x DK k30
BW k6
2 x DK k30
BW k6

You will be left with 12st wide floats (strands of yarn not included in the structure) but don't worry about these as they can be sewn in later. Try to leave a long end – it makes sewing in easier.

Rows 13–18 Continue following the yarn layout as established, knitting the even numbered rows and purling the odd numbered rows

Row 19 Changeover your yarns as you did before:

BW p18
2 x DK p6
BW p30
2 x DK p6
BW p30
2 x DK p6
BW p18

Rows 2–19 make up 1 repeat of the pattern (which should measure around 14cm long). You need to do 9 more repeats like this. Then repeat Rows 2–11 again and on the following (knit) row cast off purlwise.

We fringed the ends of ours carrying on the yarns in the pattern – see page 110 for instructions on fringing.

lacy panel

This panel uses a series of different repeats that work in order to create an impressive overall effect. As long as you complete each repeat before moving onto the next the pattern will work out. To make your piece longer you can do more of whichever repeat you like. To make it wider cast on more repeats widthways. You can create as many repeats as you like to suit your chosen space, but what we did is written in italics.

What you need

- 4mm (no 8) needles
- Patons Linen Shadow DK (we used 8 balls of colour 102)

What you do

Cast on a multiple of 24st + 7. (We cast on 79st.) You may wish to do a single repeat for a few rows first to check how wide it is – ours was 10.5cm wide + 3.5cm for the 7 edge stitches (35cm wide overall). See page 130 for instructions on KB and PB.

Row 1 purl

Row 2 purl

Section 1 (2 row repeat)

Row 1 sl1 wyib KB k1 (yo k10 sl1 wyib k2tog psso k10 yo k1) x3, k3

Row 2 sl1 wyif PB purl to end (and all other even rows in the whole pattern)

Repeat Rows 1 and 2 for desired length. Using these needles and yarn you can expect 2.4 rows per cm (we did 72 rows).

We did this section making sure the yo stitches were worked with twists to close the lace holes (see page 136). If you prefer you can work without twists to create lace holes.

Section 2 (44 row repeat)

Row 1 sl1 wyib KB k1 (yo k10 sl1 wyib k2tog psso k10 yo k1) x3, k3

Row 3 sl1 wyib KB k1 (k1 yo k9 sl1 wyib k2tog psso k9 yo k2) x3, k3

Row 5 sl1 wyib KB k1 (k2 yo k8 sl1 wyib K2tog psso k8 yo k3) x3, k3

Row 7 sl1 wyib KB k1 (k3 yo k7 sl1 wyib k2tog psso k7 yo k4) x3, k3

Row 9 sl1 wyib KB k1 (k4 yo k6 sl1 wyib k2tog psso k6 yo k5) x3, k3

Row 11 sl1 wyib KB k1 (k5 yo k5 sl1 wyib k2tog psso k5 yo k6) x3, k3

Row 13 sl1 wyib KB k1 (k6 yo k4 sl1 wyib k2tog psso k4 yo k7) x3, k3

Row 15 sl1 wyib KB k1 (k7 yo k3 sl1 wyib k2tog psso k3 yo k8) x3, k3

Row 17 sl1 wyib KB k1 (k8 yo k2 sl1 wyib k2tog psso k2 yo k9) x3, k3

Row 19 sl1 wyib KB k1 (k9 yo k1 sl1 wyib k2tog psso k1 yo k10) x3, k3

Row 21 sl1 wyib KB k1 (k10 yo sl1 wyib k2tog psso yo k11) x3, k3

Row 23 sl1 wyib KB k2tog k10 (yo k1 yo k10 sl1 wyib k2tog psso k10) x2, yo k1 yo k10 k2tog k3

Row 25 sl1 wyib KB k2tog k9 (yo k3 yo k9 sl1 wyib k2tog psso k9) x2, yo k3 yo k9 k2tog k3

Row 27 sl1 wyib KB k2tog k8 (yo k5 yo k8 sl1 wyib k2tog psso k8) x2, yo k5 yo k8 k2tog k3

Row 29 sl1 wyib KB k2tog k7 (yo k7 yo k7 sl1 wyib k2tog psso k7) x2, yo k7 yo k7 k2tog k3

Row 31 sl1 wyib KB k2tog k6 (yo k9 yo k6 sl1 wyib k2tog psso k6) x2, yo k9 yo k6 k2tog k3

Row 33 sl1 wyib KB k2tog k5 (yo k11 yo k5 sl1 wyib k2tog psso k5) x2, yo k11 yo k5 k2tog k3

Row 35 sl1 wyib KB k2tog k4 (yo k13 yo k4 sl1 wyib k2tog psso k4) x2, yo k13 yo k4 k2tog k3

Row 37 sl1 wyib KB k2tog k3 (yo k15 yo k3 sl1 wyib k2tog psso k3) x2, yo k15 yo k3 k2tog k3

continued on page 87

This lacy panel uses twisted and non-twisted yarn over stitches to great effect, creating a pattern that develops down the length of the piece and looks amazing. By referencing old-style lace café curtains this introduces a sense of the traditional but presents it from a thoroughly modern aspect.

Row 39 sl1 wyib KB k2tog k2 (yo k17 yo k2 sl1 wyib k2tog psso k2) x2, yo k17 yo k2 k2tog k3

Row 41 sl1 wyib KB k2tog k1 (yo k19 yo k1 sl1 wyib k2tog psso k1) x2, yo k19 yo k1 k2tog k3

Row 43 sl1 wyib KB k2tog (yo k21 yo sl1 wyib k2tog psso) x2, yo k21 yo k2tog k3

We did 2 repeats of this (including the one above) with the yo worked with twists to close the lace holes. We then did two repeats working them without twists.

Section 3 (20 row repeat)

Row 1 sl1 wyib KB k1 (yo k4 sl1 wyib k2tog psso k4 yo k1) x6, k3

Row 3 sl1 wyib KB k1 (k1 yo k3 sl1 wyib k2tog psso k3 yo k2) x6, k3

Row 5 sl1 wyib KB k1 (k2 yo k2 sl1 wyib k2tog psso k2 yo k3) x6, k3

Row 7 sl1 wyib KB k1 (k3 yo k1 sl1 wyib k2tog psso k1 yo k4) x6, k3

Row 9 sl1 wyib KB k1 (k4 yo sl1 wyib k2tog psso yo k5) x6, k3

Row 11 sl1 wyib KB k2tog (k4 yo k1 yo k4 sl1 wyib k2tog psso) x5, k4 yo k1 yo k4 k2tog k3

Row 13 sl1 wyib KB k2tog (k3 yo k3 yo k3 sl1 wyib k2tog psso) x5, k3 yo k3 yo k3 k2tog k3

Row 15 sl1 wyib KB k2tog (k2 yo k5 yo k2 sl1 wyib k2tog psso) x5, k2 yo k5 yo k2 k2tog k3

Row 17 sl1 wyib KB k2tog (k1 yo k7 yo k1 sl1 wyib k2tog psso) x5, k1 yo k7 yo k1 k2tog k3

Row 19 sl1 wyib KB k2tog (yo k9 yo sl1 wyib k2tog psso) x5, yo k9 yo k2tog k3

We did 2 of these repeats working the yo with no twists.

Section 4 (2 row repeat)

Row 1 sl1 wyib KB (k1 yo k4 sl1 wyib k2tog psso k4 yo) x6, k4

We repeated these two rows for 28 rows without twists in the yo.

Section 5 (8 row repeat)

Row 1 sl1 wyib KB (k1 yo k1 sl1 wyib k2tog psso k1 yo) x12, k1 k3

Row 3 sl1 wyib KB (k2 yo sl1 wyib k2tog psso yo k1) x12, k4

Row 5 sl1 wyib KB k2tog (k1 yo k1 yo k1 sl1 wyib k2tog psso) x11, k1 yo k1 yo k1 k2tog k3

Row 7 sl1 wyib KB k2tog (yo k3 yo sl1 wyib k2tog psso) x11, yo k3 yo k2tog k3

We repeated this section 3 times (including this repeat) without twists and 3 repeats with twists.

Section 6 (2 row repeat)

Row 1 sl1 wyib KB (k1 yo k1 sl1 wyib k2tog psso k1 yo) x12, k4

We repeated these 2 rows for 48 rows with twists.

To finish

Row 1 knit
Row 2 purl
Row 3 knit
Row 4 purl
Row 5 knit

On the next row (which should be a purl row) cast off knitwise.

Our panel is 35cm wide x 165cm long.

When you've finished you need to give your panel a good steam (see page 140). Then find a thin piece of wooden dowel the same length as the width of your piece and lay it against the top plain section of the panel. Wrap the top over the dowel and sew it down. You can then put a hanging loop in and hang your panel.

There is something very comforting about interiors with knitted details. They add a certain warmth and charm so welcome in a home. However it is likely that most things you have already will not be knitted, so it's really important you consider how your lovely knit will fit in to your existing space so it works as a whole.

BESPOKE KNITTING FOR YOUR HOME

Luckily it's really easy to work out how to cover something with a bit of measuring and some simple maths – it's only a small step from everything covered so far in this book. The key now though is proper planning and thought for the design of your piece – if you're covering a chair, for example, it will take a long time, use a lot of yarn and you will have to live with it when it's finished. I strongly recommend taking time to consider how the colour, texture and pattern will work within the room. Using your samples try your ideas out in the space before getting started. Remember, if you're doing something big a strong design will be far more dominant on that scale instead of the small swatch you have in your hand so imagination and vision are vital at this point. Sometimes photographs of your space can help reduce the scale and show more easily how your new design will fit in scale wise. You can use whatever technique you find helpful to visualize the finished result – just go for it.

doorstop

Although extremely easy this is the perfect introduction to creating a knit that fits a solid object. It also introduces the idea of knitting with tougher materials – a perfect alternative for items where conventional yarns aren't as suitable.

What you need

- something square and heavy to cover (we used a piece of wood)
- 7 to 10mm (no 2 to 000) needles (the exact size is up to you)
- some chunky yarn (*we used Rowan Big Wool in colour 001*)
- some raffia or something similar

OBJECTS MADE OF SQUARES OR RECTANGLES

If the object you wish to cover is made up of flat sides with right angles then you can use everything you've learnt to work out each panel, which when sewn together will fit snugly. Now is when you need to think about what the edges of any open sides will look like and where you want to place your patterns on the object. Take it bit by bit and you'll be fine.

What you do

Measure each side of your block and work out how many stitches and rows you need for each panel, using your stitch tension worked out from a sample as described on page 138. You can then either knit each panel individually and sew each side up or add some together (for example, the four around the outside could be knitted in one strip) so you have fewer seams. If your knit is open and exposes the block, you may need to paint the block or make a fabric cover of the same or a contrasting colour to show through the knit.

Our version has a 17cm square cube and has the following panels:

Panel 1

Using Big Wool cast on 21st and alternate knit and purl for 24 rows.

Panels 2, 3 and 4

Using Big Wool cast on 21st wide and alternate knit and purl for 12 rows. Change to raffia and continue for another 12 rows.

Panel 5

Using raffia cast on 21st and alternate knit and purl for 24 rows.

We added a tough hessian panel on the base but you could do another of the panels with both yarns and it could be used any way up. Simply sew the panels together and pull over the block before sewing it in.

cabled footstool

To complement more traditional furniture you might consider a busy pattern like this. However, if your taste is more simple then you can pare it down as you like. This footstool is essentially made of flat panels like the doorstop, albeit far more complicated ones.

What you need

- 4mm (no 8) needles
- a cable needle
- Rowan British Sheep Breeds (*we used about 4 balls of colour 780 Ecru*)
- a footstool

The footstool we used measured 40cm x 30cm around the top and approximately 8cm high. This is a standard size but you can always alter the size of the pieces (quantity of cables/repeats and so on) to make yours fit.

Each panel uses a variety of stitches and was worked out in the same way as the bolster cushion (see pages 68–73), demonstrating how, by combining techniques, you can create an impressive design step by step. The full drawings and calculations are shown on page 141 for your reference.

See page 130 for instructions on KB and PB.

What you do

The top

Ours measured 39cm wide x 29cm long

Cast on 126st

Row 1 purl

Row 2 purl

Row 3 sl1 wyib (KB) x12, k76 (KB) x12, k1

Row 4 (and all other even rows) sl1 wyif p1 (PB) x11, p78 (PB) x11, p2

Row 5 sl1 wyib (KB) x12, k1 (sl2 to cn, hold in back, k2, k2 from cn; this is called 4st Cable Back) k66 (sl2 to cn, hold in front, k2, k2 from cn; this is called 4st Cable Front) k1 (KB) x12, k1

Row 7 sl 1 wyib (KB) x12, k6 (sl4 to cn, hold in back, k4, k4 from cn; this is called 8st Cable Back) x8, k6 (KB) x12, k1

Row 9 as Row 5

Row 11 as Row 3

Row 13 sl1 wyib (KB) x12, k1 4st Cable Back k5 (sl4 to cn, hold in front, k4, k4 from cn; this is called 8st Cable Front) x7, k5 4st Cable Front k1 (KB) x12, k1

Rows 15–86 repeat Rows 3–14

Rows 87–94 repeat Rows 3–10

Cast off purlwise

The side trim

Ours measured 7cm wide x 138cm long

Cast on 24st

Row 1 purl

Row 2 purl

Row 3 sl1 wyib KB k13 (sl2 wyib k2) x2

Row 4 sl1 wyif p1 sl2 wyif p2 sl2 wyif, purl to end

Row 5 sl1 wyib KB k12 (sl1 to cn, hold in back, k1, k1 from cn, sl1 to cn, hold in front, k1, k1 from cn; this is called Small Bird Cable) x2, k1

Row 6 sl1 wyif, purl to end

Row 7 sl1 wyib KB (sl3 to cn, hold in back, k3, k3 from cn, sl3 to cn, hold in front, k3, k3 from cn; this is called Double Cable Pointing Down) k1 (sl2 wyib k2) x2

Row 8 as Row 4

Row 9 as Row 5

Row 10 as Row 6

Row 11 as Row 3

continued on page 97

Row 12 as Row 4

Row 13 sl1 wyib KB Double Cable Pointing Down (Small Bird Cable) x2, k1

Row 14 as Row 6

Row 15 – 62 repeat Rows 3–14 Continue to repeat Rows 3–6, working (sl3 to cn, hold in front, k3, k3 from cn, sl3 to cn, hold in back, k3, k3 from cn; this is called Double Cable Pointing Up) or Double Cable Pointing Down on the indicated rows

Double cable pointing up

Rows 77, 83, 89, 95, 101, 107, 113, 119, 125, 131

End of section 1 Row 135 (39.5cm)

Double cable pointing down

Rows 139, 145, 151, 157, 163, 169, 175, 181

End of section 2a Row 185 (52cm)

Double cables pointing up

Rows 189, 195, 201, 207, 213, 219, 225, 231

End of section 2b Row 235 (69cm)

Double cable pointing down

Rows 239, 245, 251, 257, 263, 269, 275, 281, 287, 293

End of section 3a Row 301 (86.5cm)

Double cable pointing up

Rows 309, 315, 321, 327, 333, 339, 345, 351, 357, 363

End of section 3b Row 367 (108.5cm)

Double cable pointing down

Rows 371, 377, 383, 389, 395, 401, 407, 413

End of section 4a Row 417 (120cm)

Double cable pointing up

Rows 421, 427, 433, 439, 445, 451, 457, 463

End of piece Row 465 (134.5cm)

Cast off knitwise

Sew the ends of the side trim together first, then match up the corner details of this strip to the corners of the top and sew the two parts together. We pulled our cover on and sewed a line of running stitches around the hem to fix it to the stool securely, but if you just want to pull it on then make your side trim a bit wider and shorter than the stool and it will cling on.

cushions for chairs

To make this chair cover we designed it bit by bit. Generally it is easier to pick furniture with removable pads so you can measure them and fit the knitted covers more easily. For this chair we kept it simple and made two panels the same width, one long enough to stretch up and over the back and the other to cover the top, front and back edges of the seat pad. Measure each part you want to cover and work out the panel width accordingly. You can work out the length at this stage or just keep knitting until it's long enough.

What you need
• 6.5mm (no 3) needles
• cable needle
• Rowan Felted Tweed Chunky (*we used 12 balls 283 Grey Pebble*)

What you do
The cable section is a fixed pattern and is 19cm wide, but you can adapt the width of the edge – the stitch tension for this is 12st/10cm. (*we used 19 sts for each edge*)

Chair Back
Cast on necessary number of sts (*we cast on 72 sts*)
Row 1 purl
Row 2 purl
Row 3 (purl number of stitches you are using for the bumpy edge then turn your piece, knit the same number of stitches, turn, purl same stitches, turn, knit same stitches, turn, look over your piece to the back and use your right needle to pick up the purl stitch directly below the first stitch on your left needle, lift this stitch up onto your left needle and knit this and the original first stitch together; repeat this for all your edge stitches; this is called Ridge) k34 (Ridge)
Row 4 purl
Row 5 knit Ridge st k1 (sl4 to cn, hold in back, k4, k4 from cn; this is called 8st Cable Back) x2, (sl4 to cn, hold in front, k4, k4 from cn; this is called 8st Cable Front) x2, k1 knit Ridge st
Row 6 purl
Row 7 (Ridge) k34 (Ridge)
Row 8 purl
Row 9 knit
Row 10 purl
Row 11 (Ridge) k5 (8st Cable Front) k8 (8st Cable Back) k5 (Ridge)
Row 12 purl
Row 13 knit
Row 14 purl
Row 15 (Ridge) k34 (Ridge)
Row 16 purl

Rows 5–16 is one repeat – do as many of these as you need.

For the seat pad we made a plain piece of knitting big enough to cover the base and the sides. The base was 62cm wide x 48cm long. The seat pad was 7cm thick. It needed to be 76cm wide x 48cm for a snug fit. Reduce your total slightly when you've worked out what you need to achieve this.

The tension we used for our plain section was 1.33st x 1.5r/cm.

Place the pieces on your cushion pads and check they fit. Pin them together with safety pins and either sew them together from the outside while on the cushion or slip them off, turn inside out and sew up as normal leaving one seam open (the least visible when you put it back on the chair). Pull the cover over and sew the last seam from the outside. If you would like to remove your covers then use this seam to add buttons or poppers.

The rich texture of the knit works so well in this minimal space because the pattern is so strong, reflecting the lines of the room.

circular place mat

This project is one that looks really impressive but is actually easy to knit. Once you've got the hang of the theory of knitting curves you could use it for all sorts of items – not just our stylish reinvention of the humble doily!

What you need

- 4mm (size 8) needles
- Rowan Pima Cotton DK (*we used 2 balls of colour 057*)

SHAPING TO FIT CURVES

So far almost everything has been a variation of a square – flat with right angles and perfect for knit's grid-like structure. However, to fit different shapes you need to know how to shape your knitting. Basically this is done by decreasing or increasing a certain number of stitches on particular rows to grow and shrink your knitting according to the shape you want. To work out what to do, you need to measure your item and make a plan of it on some paper. This doesn't have to be to scale, as long as the measurements are right. See the instructions on pages 142–43 to see how to convert these drawings into pattern instructions.

What you do

Cast on 24st

Row 1 purl

Row 2 (p1 yo p1 yo p1) x8 (40st)

Row 3 Double length knit (put your needle through to knit as normal but wind yarn around twice instead of once; work as a normal stitch on next row, which will release the long stitch)

Row 4 knit

Row 5 knit

Row 6 p1 (p2tog yo) to last st, p1

Row 7 purl

Row 8 (p1 yo p1 yo p1 yo p1 yo p1) x8 (72st)

Rows 9 – 15 repeat Rows 1–7 with the following exception: the equivalent to Row 2 is just purl with no yo from now on.

Row 16 (p1 yo p2 yo p1 yo p1 yo p1 yo p2 yo p1) x8 (120st)

Rows 17 – 23 repeat Rows 9 – 15

Row 24 (p2 yo p2 yo p2 yo p3 yo p2 yo p2 yo p2) x8 (168st)

Rows 25 – 31 repeat Rows 9 – 15

Row 32 (p3 yo p3 yo p3 yo p3 yo p3 yo p3 yo p3) x8 (216st)

Rows 33 – 39 repeat Rows 9 – 15

Row 40 (p4 yo p4 yo p4 yo p3 yo p4 yo p4 yo p4) x8 (264st)

Rows 41 – 47 repeat Rows 9 – 15

Row 48 (p4 yo p5 yo p5 yo p5 yo p5 yo p5 yo p4) x8 (312st)

Rows 49 – 55 repeat Rows 9 – 15

Row 56 (p6 yo p6 yo p5 yo p5 yo p5 yo p6 yo p6) x8 (360st)

Row 57 purl

Row 58 cast off knitwise

Your cast-on measurement should be 11cm. The length of each repeat should be 3.5cm. Each repeat should add an extra 21.5cm to the width of the piece. When you've knitted it simply fold it in half widthways, right sides together and sew down the seam. If you would like a bigger circle just continue knitting, increasing as shown with each repeat. Once your circle is sewn together then give it a steam on the reverse (see page 140) and it will look lovely.

When you've made
this once you'll realize
that with this pattern
you can easily adapt it
to make small circles
for coasters, great big
ones for tablecloths or
at the other end of the
scale alter your yarn to
something substantial
and increase your
needle size to make
a rug – you just need
really long circular
needles to hold all the
stitches comfortably.

round pouffe

For this project we found a Moroccan-style pouffe sized approximately 54cm across by 30cm high. For a snug fit we made the cover a bit smaller – 52cm across x 24cm high. As the knit is pulled tight the inside may show, so use a pouffe a similar colour to the yarn.

What you need

- 9mm (no 00) circular needles
- a cable needle
- Patons Wool Blend Aran (*we used 8 balls of colour 88*)
- 3 large poppers

What you do

Cast on 62st using 3 strands of the yarn held together

Row 1 purl

Row 2 purl

Row 3 sl1 wyib k1 (k1 yo k4) x12 (74st)

We worked the yo with a twist – if you work without you will get lace holes (see page 136).

Rows 4 – 38 even rows sl1 wyif, purl to end

Row 5 sl1 wyib k1 (k5 yo k1) x12 (86st)

Row 7 sl1 wyib k1 (k1 yo k6) x12 (98st)

Row 9 sl1 wyib k1 (k7 yo k1) x12 (110st)

Row 11 sl1 wyib k1 (k1 yo k8) x12 (122st)

Row 13 sl1 wyib k1 (k9 yo k1) x12 (134st)

Row 15 sl1 wyib k1 (k1 yo k10) x12 (148st)

Row 17 sl1 wyib k1 (k11 yo k1) x12 (158st)

Row 19 sl1 wyib k1 (k1 yo k12) x12 (170st)

Row 21 cast off 2 st purlwise, knit to end (168 sts)

Rows 23, 25 sl1 wyib, knit to end

Rows 27, 29, 31, 33 sl1 wyib (k2 p3) x33, k2

Row 35 sl1 wyib (KB k2) x41, KB k1

Row 37 sl1 wyib (k1 KB k1) x41, k3

Row 39 sl1 wyib (k2 KB) x41, k3

Row 40 sl1 wyif (p2 PB) x41, p3

Rows 41, 43, 45 sl1 wyib, knit to end

Row 42 sl1 wyif p1 (p2 PB) x41, p2

Row 44 sl1 wyif (PB p2) x41, PB, p1

Rows 45, 47, 49, 51, 53 sl1 wyib knit to end

Rows 46, 48, 50, 52 sl1 wyif p1 (k3 p2) x33, p1

Row 53 sl1 wyib yo knit to last st yo k1 (170st)

Rows 54 – 72 even rows sl1 wyif, purl to end

Row 55 sl1 wyib [(sl2 to cn, hold in front, k2, k2 from cn; this is called 4st Cable Front) k4 k2tog k4]

x12, k1 (158st)

Row 57 sl1 wyib (k8 k2tog k3) x12, k1 (146st)

Row 59 sl1 wyib (4st Cable Front k3 k2tog k3) x12, k1 (134st)

Row 61 sl1 wyib (k7 k2tog k2) x12, k1 (122sts)

Row 63 sl1 wyib (4st Cable Front k2 k2tog k2) x12, k1 (110sts)

Row 65 sl1 wyib (k6 k2tog k1) x12, k1 (98st)

Row 67 sl1 wyib (4st Cable Front k1 k2tog k1) x12, k1 (86st)

Row 69 sl1 wyib (k5 k2tog) x12, k1 (74st)

Row 71 sl1 wyib (4st Cable Front k2tog) x12, k1 (62st)

Row 73 sl1 wyib, purl to end

Row 74 double length p2tog (put your needle through to p2tog as normal but wind yarn around twice instead of once; work as a normal stitch on next row, which will release the long stitch) – repeat to end (31st)

Row 75 purl

Row 76 double length p2tog –repeat to end (16st)

Row 77 purl

continued on page 109

Row 78 (sl1 wyif k2tog psso) x 5, p1

Row 79 pull a long length of yarn through 6 remaining stitches, gather them together and sew yarn through stitches twice more to create a firm finish. Fold your piece in half lengthways, right sides together and sew the seam down to row 22. Fold the plain strip down to the cast on back on itself – this is your band to sew one half of the poppers onto. Sew the matching halves onto the other edge.

This contemporary space has lots of contrasting materials and textures, but by keeping the muted colour palette simple they work together, creating extra warmth. Featured alongside the Pouffe are the Geometric Cable Throw (see pages 62–65) and the Intarsia Blanket (see pages 80–83).

COLOUR CONTRAST

We used a silver coloured pouffe under grey wool so that the pouffe didn't show through. However, if you are feeling adventurous you could use could use this as a feature and introduce a contrasting colour – hot pink or orange under grey would be good.

Although knitting is frankly pretty incredible, there are times when you might fancy adding something else when you've finished the knitting bit, or shaping the knitting to create three-dimensional structure with the fabric itself. Once you're comfortable with the basic process you can start to question it and the application of knit within your home. While clearly functional there is no reason why it can't be thought of as purely decorative, acting almost as a piece of art in its own right – or at the opposite end of the scale as tough and practical, such as the Ridge Rug (see pages 120–23). There really are very few limits and hopefully this chapter will help show you what can be possible with a bit of imagination.

ADDING EMBELLISHMENTS AND EXTRA TEXTURE

An old favourite and one of the easiest embellishments is fringing – you just fold a piece of yarn in half and thread the fold from front to back through the edge then pull the free ends through the fold. Basically that's it. If you want a lot the same size, wrap your fringing yarn around a book or something similar that is the right width for the fringing you want – just cut along one edge and there you have it. If you want them all the same length you'll invariably need to give it a haircut when you've finished the fringing, or you could intentionally leave it all different lengths. We use a lot of fringing, which I'm sure you can spot throughout the book – each example perfect for that specific project.

seascape wall hanging

This is one of my favourite pieces in this book – it's so heavy there is something very reassuring about its presence. In terms of knitting it's not massively difficult, but it will take a long time and some very tough, long circular needles. However, as I'm sure you'll agree the structure that is formed has so much movement and life that it really does present this ancient craft in a new light.

What you need
- size 7mm (no 2) circular needles
- about 2 kilos of yarn (*we used all sorts of yarns of a chunky weight or knitted with 2 or 3 balls of finer weight yarn*)
- a piece of wooden dowel 1.2m long x 2.5cm diameter

CREATING TEXTURE WITHIN THE STRUCTURE OF THE KNIT ITSELF

There are two ways of creating texture, on a small scale through the use of different yarns or stitches, or on a big scale through building shape into the structure. By excessively increasing or decreasing in specific areas you will blow out or suck in the structure and can create all kinds of striking effects. The whole theory is very unpredictable though and depends enormously on exactly what you do – it's a perfect chance to really explore how yarn and stitch behave and affect each other.

What you do

The repeat is 6st wide and varies in length as you continue through the piece. Colour changes are entirely up to you but to get a similar look to ours the colour needs to be altered gradually. When you're changing to a new colour, do part of a row then reintroduce the last yarn occasionally; by avoiding a regular method you'll avoid blocks of colour, which will make the piece lose its organic feel. You could just use one colour throughout, which will give a cleaner feel. See page 130 for instructions on KB and PB.

Cast on 120st
Rows 1–2 purl
Row 3 knit
Row 4 purl
Row 5 sl1 wyib KB ([insert your right needle under the yarn that joins the stitches on either needle and pick it up so it looks like a yo; this is called pick up] k1 KB k1 KB) x19, pick up k1 KB (140st)
Row 6 sl1 wyif PB (p2 PB p1 PB) x19, p2 PB
Row 7 sl1 wyib KB (yo k1 yo k1 KB k1 KB) x19, yo k1 yo k1 KB (180 t)
Row 8 sl1 wyif PB (p4 PB p1 PB) x19, p4 PB
Row 9 sl1 wyib KB (yo k3 yo k1 KB k1 KB) x19, yo k3 yo k1 KB (220st)
Rows 10, 12, 14 repeat Row 8, working 2 additional purl sts each row, in place of p4
Row 11 sl1 wyib KB (yo k5 yo k1 KB k1 KB) x19, yo k5 yo k1 KB (260st)
Row 13 sl1 wyib KB (yo k7 yo k1 KB k1 KB) x19, yo k7 yo k1 KB (300st)
Row 15 sl1 wyib KB (k3 [sl1 wyib k2tog psso; this is called sk2p] k4 KB pick up k1 KB) x19, k3 sk2p k4 KB (279st)
Row 16 sl1 wyif PB (p8 PB p2 PB) x19, p8 PB
Row 17 sl1 wyib KB (k2 sk2p k3 KB yo k1 yo k1 KB) x19, k2 sk2p k3 KB (277st)
Row 18 sl1 wyif PB (p6, PB, p4, PB) x19, p6, PB

continued on page 114

Row 19 sl1 wyib KB (k1 sk2p k2 KB yo k3 yo k1 KB) x19, k1 sk2p k2 KB (275st)

Row 20 sl1 wyif PB (p4, PB, p6, PB) x19, p4, PB

Row 21 sl1 wyib KB (sk2p k1 KB yo k5 yo k1 KB) x19, sk2p k1 KB (273st)

Row 22 sl1 wyif PB (p2tog PB p8 PB) x19, p2tog PB (253st)

Row 23 sl1 wyib KB (k1 KB yo k7 yo k1 KB) x19, k1 KB (291st)

Row 24 sl1 wyif PB (p1 PB p10 PB) x19, p1 PB

Row 25 sl1 wyib KB (k1 KB yo k9 yo k1 KB) x19, k1 KB (329st)

Row 26 sl1 wyif PB (p1 PB p12 PB) x19, p1 PB

Row 27 sl1 wyib KB (pick up k1 KB k4 sk2p k5 KB) x19, pick up k1 KB (311st)

Row 28 sl1 wyif PB (p2 PB p10 PB) x19, p2 PB

Row 29 sl1 wyib KB (yo k1 yo k1 KB k3 sk2p k4 KB) x19, yo k1 yo k1 KB (313st)

Row 30 sl1 wyif PB (p4 PB p8 PB) x19, p4 PB

Row 31 sl1 wyib KB (yo k3 yo k1 KB k2 sk2p k3 KB) x19, yo k3 yo k1 KB (315st)

Row 32 sl1 wyif PB (p6 PB) x39

Row 33 sl1 wyib KB (yo k5 yo k1 KB k1 sk2p k2 KB) x19, yo k5 yo k1 KB (317st)

Row 34 sl1 wyif PB (p8 PB p4 PB) x19, p8 PB

Row 35 sl1 wyib KB (yo k7 yo k1 KB sk2p k1 KB) x19, yo k7 yo k1 KB (319st)

Row 36 sl1 wyif PB (p10 PB p2tog PB) x19, p10 PB (300st)

Row 37 sl1 wyib KB (yo k9 yo k1 KB k1 KB) x19, yo k9 yo k1 KB (340st)

Row 38 sl1 wyif PB (p12 PB p1 PB) x19, p12 PB

Row 39 sl1 wyib KB (yo k11 yo k1 KB k1 KB) x19, yo k11 yo k1 KB (380st)

Row 40 sl1 wyif PB (p14 PB p1 PB) x19, p14 PB

Row 41 sl1 wyib KB (k5 sk2p k6 KB k1 KB) x19, k5 sk2p k6 KB (340st)

Row 42 as Row 38

Row 43 sl1 wyib KB (k4 sk2p k5 KB k1 KB) x19, k4 sk2p k5 KB (300st)

Row 44 sl1 wyif PB (p10 PB p1 PB) x19, p10 PB

Row 45 sl1 wyib KB (k3 sk2p k4 KB pick up k1 KB) x19, k3 sk2p k4 KB (279st)

Row 46 sl1 wyif PB (p8 PB yo p1 yo p1 PB) x19, p8 PB (317st)

Row 47 sl1 wyib KB (k2 sk2p k3 KB yo k3 yo k1 KB) x19, k2 sk2p k3 KB (315st)

Rows 48, 50 repeat Row 46 purling 2 less sts between PBs and purling 4 additional sts between yos each row (38st increased each row)

Rows 49, 51 repeat Row 47 knitting 1 less st each side of sk2p and 4 additional sts between yos each row (2st decreased each row; 387st after Row 51)

Row 52 sl1 wyif PB (p2tog PB yo p13 yo p1 PB) x19, p2tog PB (405st)

Row 53 sl1 wyib KB (k1 KB yo k15 yo k1 KB) x19, k1 KB (443st)

Row 54 sl1 wyif PB (p1 PB yo p17 yo p1 PB) x19, p1 PB (481st)

Row 55 sl1 wyib KB (k1 KB yo k19 yo k1 KB) x19, k1 KB (519st)

Row 56 sl1 wyif PB (p1 PB yo p21 yo p1 PB) x19, p1 PB (557st)

Row 57 sl1 wyib KB (k1 KB k10 sk2p k11 KB) x19, k1 KB (519st)

Row 58 sl1 wyif PB (p1 PB p22 PB) x19 p1 PB

Rows 59, 61, 63, 65 repeat Row 57 knitting 1 less st each side of sk2p each row (38st decreased each row; 367st after Row 65)

Rows 60, 62, 64, 66 repeat Row 58, working 2 fewer purl sts each row, in place of p22

Row 67 sl1 wyib KB (pick up the yarn between the stitches in the row below and knit it, making sure there is a twist in the yarn k1 KB k5 sk2p k6 KB) x19, pick up as before k1 KB (349st)

Row 68 sl1 wyif PB (yo p1 yo p1 PB p12 PB) x19, yo p1 yo p1 PB (389st)

Row 69 sl1 wyib KB (yo k3 yo k1 KB k4 sk2p k5 KB) x19, yo k3 yo k1 KB (391st)

Rows 70, 72, 74, 76 repeat Row 68, purling 2 less sts between PBs and an additional 4st between yos each row (40sts increased each row)

Rows 71, 73, 75, 77 repeat Row 69, knitting 1 less st each side of sk2p and 4 additional sts between yos each row (2st increased each row; 559st after Row 77)

Row 78 sl1 wyif PB (yo p21 yo p1 PB p2tog PB) x19, yo p21 yo p1 PB (580st)

Row 79 sl1 wyib KB (yo k23 yo k1 KB k1 KB) x19, yo k23 yo k1 KB (620st)

Row 80 sl1 wyif PB (p26 PB p1 PB) x19, p26 PB

Row 81 sl1 wyib KB (k11 sk2p k12 KB k1 KB) x19, k11 sk2p k12 KB (580st)

Rows 82, 84, 86, 88, 90, 92 repeat Row 80, working 2 fewer purl sts each row, in place of p26

Rows 83, 85, 87, 89, 91 repeat Row 81 knitting 1 less st each side of sk2p each row (40st decreased each row; 380st after Row 91)

Row 93 sl1 wyib KB (k5 sk2p k6 KB pick up k1 KB) x19, k5 sk2p k6 KB (359st)

Row 94 sl1 wyif PB (p12 PB yo p1 yo p1 PB) x19, p12 PB (397st)

Row 95 sl1 wyib KB (k4 sk2p k5 KB yo k3 yo k1 KB) x19, k4 sk2p k5 KB (395st)

Rows 96, 98, 100, 102 repeat Row 94 purling 2 less sts between PBs and 4 additional sts between yos each row (38st increased each row)

Rows 97, 99, 101, 103 repeat Row 95 knitting 1 less st each side of sk2p and 4 additional sts between yos each row (2st decreased each row; 539st after Row 103)

Row 104 sl1 wyif PB (p2tog PB yo p21 yo p1 PB) x19, p2tog PB (557st)

Row 105 sl1 wyib KB (k1 KB yo k23 yo k1 KB) x19, k1 KB (595st)

Row 106 sl1 wyif PB (p1 PB yo p25 yo p1 PB) x19, p1 PB (633st)

Row 107 sl1 wyib KB (k1 KB yo k27 yo k1 KB) x19, k1 KB (671st)

Row 108 sl1 wyif PB (p1 PB yo p29 yo p1 PB) x19, p1 PB (709st)

Row 109 sl1 wyib KB (k1 KB k14 sk2p k15 KB) x19, k1 KB (671st)

Row 110 sl1 wyif PB (p1 PB p30, PB) x19, p1 PB

Rows 111, 113, 115, 117, 119, 121, 123, 125 repeat Row 109, knitting 1 less st each side of sk2p each row (38st decreased each row; 367st after Row 125)

Rows 112, 114, 116, 118, 120, 122, 124, 126 repeat Row 110, purling 2 less sts each row in place of p30

Repeat Rows 67–103 (or if you want to make your hanging longer Rows 67–126 is a full repeat)

Cast off knitwise

Fold the top edge over the dowel and sew in place.

ridge rug

This rug is entirely adaptable to whatever size you need, it's wonderfully springy and if you use some tough yarn it will be fairly hard-wearing too. The pattern is easy to add stripes into and simple to do once you've got the hang of it. Ours is pretty uncomplicated and looks really chic as a result.

What you need

- 9mm (no 00) needles
- Patons Wool Blend Aran (*we held 2 ends of each colour together and used two colours: 13 balls of shade 10 dark brown for the main colour [Col A] and 7 balls of shade 14 marled brown [Col B]*).

What you do

The stitch tension for our rug is 1 repeat/2cm. Our rug was 87st wide (92cm) x 70 repeats.

Cast on using however many stitches you need for the size of rug you want using two balls of Col A

Row 1 purl (Col A)

Row 2 purl (Col A)

Row 3 knit (Col B)

Row 4 purl (Col B)

Row 5 knit (Col B)

Row 6 knit (Col A)

Row 7 purl (Col A)

Row 8 knit (Col A)

Row 9 purl (Col A)

Row 10 using Col B look at the front of your piece and using the right needle hook the Col B purled stitch a few rows directly below the next stitch up onto the left needle, then purl this and the original first stitch together. Repeat this all along the row.

Rows 3–10 is one repeat so just do as many as you need.

To finish, using Col A do one row purl then cast off knitwise.

The squishy ridges
this rug is made up
of provide an inviting
contrast of warmth
against the polished
concrete floor.

woven wall hanging

This is a deceptively simple design that uses a lot of weaving. We used a selection of yarns that are off-white in colour but you could substitute any yarns of approximately the same weight as the ones we used.

What you need
- 10mm (no 000) circular needles
- Rowan Big Wool (4 balls)
- Debbie Bliss Rialto Chunky (3 balls)
- Debbie Bliss Donegal Luxury Tweed Chunky (1 ball)
- Debbie Bliss Amalfi (paler colour x 4, darker colour x 3)
- Rowan British Sheep Breeds DK (2 balls)
- white willow sticks 150cm long
- flat paper tape 4mm x 15m
- 2 pieces of wooden dowel 100cm long painted the same colour/s as the first and last 8 rows

What you do
Cast on 101st using Big Wool

Rows 1–10 knit odd rows, purl even rows

Row 11 k7, introduce 1 end of paler Amalfi with 1 of Rialto and p87, take another ball of Big Wool and k7

Row 12 throughout this pattern always follow the yarn layout in the row below until instructed otherwise. Change between yarns using the intarsia method as described on page 140. p7 double length purl (put your needle through to purl as normal but wind yarn around twice instead of once; work as a normal stitch on next row, which will release the long stitch) x87, p7

Row 13 k7 turn piece p7 turn again k7 p87 k7 turn piece p7 turn piece k7 (These 'edge only' rows allow space for the long stitches.)

Rows 14–27 repeat Rows 12 and 13

Row 28 purl using Big Wool across the whole row

Row 29 k7, introduce Donegal p87, using separate ball Big Wool k7

Row 30 p7 k87 p7

Rows 31–34 repeat Rows 29–30

Row 35 as Row 29

Row 36 as Row 28

Row 37 k7 p87 k7

Row 38 p7 double length purl x 87 p7

Row 39 k7 turn piece p7 turn again k7 p87, introduce separate ball Big Wool k7 turn piece p7 turn piece, taking previous ball Big Wool k7

Rows 40–49 repeat Rows 38 and 39

Row 50 purl

Row 51 knit

Row 52 purl

Row 53 k7, introduce Donegal p87, introduce separate ball Big Wool k7

Row 54 p7 k87 p7

Row 55 knit using Big Wool

Row 56 purl

Rows 57–64 repeat Rows 55 and 56

Row 65 k7 p87 k7

Row 66 p7, taking 2 ends of paler Amalfi and 1 of Rowan DK p87, taking a new ball of Big Wool p7

Row 67 k7 k87 k7

Row 68 p7, introduce 3 ends of darker Amalfi p87, using the Big Wool as in row below p7

Row 69 k7 k1 (yo k2tog) x 43 k7

Rows 70–79 repeat Rows 66–67

Rows 80–139 repeat Rows 68–79

Rows 140–143 repeat Rows 68–71

Row 144 purl using Big Wool

Row 145 knit

Rows 146–151 repeat Rows 144–145

Row 152 cast off knitwise

Steam the hanging (see page 140), wrap the dowels in the first and last 8 rows and sew them in. Add loops and hang it while you weave the willow and paper strips horizontally and vertically into the various gaps.

Here you can see the detail of the paper and willow woven in the knitted holes. You can intentionally add lace holes to anything with a view to weaving them later – it's a simple but effective technique.

Knitting is exactly like baking; there are a few ingredients that can be combined in a million different ways to create endless possibilities. This section covers the step by step of how each knitting 'ingredient' is made to help you on your way. Although basic knitting and purling are simple to do you'd be surprised at how many small variations there are, each having a slightly different effect on the overall piece. Because hand knitting is passed from person to person, each of us assumes we all do it the same, but I've worked with so many knitters over the years that I now know if you gave 50 people the same yarn and pattern, you'd get 50 slightly different items back!

THE ESSENTIALS

I have included here step by step instructions for how I personally do everything, plus some other popular techniques. My knit stitches in particular are different from those of a lot of other people and there are subtle differences in some of the other techniques too. I was taught to knit like this and find it a simple method. It's especially good as it creates quite a loose fabric, the stitches of which are easier to play around with and manipulate (when you've got the hang of the basics) and want to push the technique further.

If you can already knit in your own way then the majority of the patterns here will work out just fine, however some of the ones that involve working the stitches in a particular way (keep an eye open for baskets, extra long stitches and yos in particular) may need you to refer to my method if yours isn't quite the same, or if the pattern isn't doing what you expected! Everyone is individual, so do whatever works best for you. Hopefully this book has inspired you to realize there is no 'right' way and by exploring different options you may discover something new along the way.

abbreviations

k knit

p purl

st stitch/es

k2tog/p2tog knit 2 stitches together/purl two stitches together

sl slip
Often the first stitch in a row is slipped to give a good edge, especially if it's going to be a raw edge and not sewn into a seam, such as on a blanket

wyib/wyif with yarn in back/ with yarn in front

psso pass the slipped stitch over

yo yarn over

KB/PB knit basket/purl basket. To make these you basically work the second stitch first, then the first and slip both off together. This only works if you knit and purl as I do, so check my instructions. When knitting, go behind the work to get to the second stitch, for purling go in front.

st/cm stitches per centimetre, or the tension

r/cm rows per centimetre

cn is a double-pointed needle used for making cables. Some people like them – some don't, I've written both methods for you (see Cables page 137)

DK double knit (weight of yarn)

casting on

Knit-on cast on

There are many ways to cast on – this is the way I do it.

Put your needles together and tie the yarn around them. Cross your needles so the right is behind the left (1). Hold the left needle like a spoon along with the short tail end of the yarn. Use your left

Long tail cast on

This method is also known as continental cast-on or double cast on. Place a slip loop on the right needle, with a tail three times the width of your cast on. Hold the ball and tail ends in the left hand and wrap the tail end round the thumb (1). Lift you ball end with your forefinger and insert the tip of the needle into the strand at the front of the thumb and through the strand on the forefinger from top to bottom (2). Bring the strand on the forefinger through the strand on the thumb to make a stitch (3).

Single thumb cast on

Also known as backward loop, Provincial or twisted loop cast on, this uses a single needle. Place a slip loop on the right needle – this is your first stitch. Close the fingers of the left hand over the yarn, with the end attached to the needle held between thumb and forefinger. Move the tumb from left to right under the needle end of the yarn and wrap it around the thumb. Insert the needle through the strand on the thumb and transfer the loop to the needle. Tighten and continue.

fforefinger and thumb to hold the cross in the needles while your right hand takes the yarn behind and then back between the needles (2). Keep your left hand firm and holding the yarn and needle in your right hand keep the yarn taught. Move the right needle back through the loop towards you, bringing the yarn wrapped around it through the loop too (3,4). Using your right needle place this new loop back on the left needle. Do this so the right needle is behind the left and ready to make the next stitch (5). Repeat this for as many stitches as you need.

Above: Long tail cast on
Below: Single thumb cast on

knit

There are many ways to knit, this is how I do it (some people call this 'through back loop') and all the instructions in this book that include 'knit' refer to this method. I use it all the time as it is how I learnt and I find working the stitches like this allows me to manipulate them more easily. My 'knit' is basically the same as my cast on, except instead of placing the loop you've pulled through (1) back on the left needle, you use it to pull the stitch it came through off the left needle (2). This is one stitch knitted. You can then move onto the next (3) and continue until you've 'knitted' all the stitches you want (4, 5).

purl

To 'purl' I insert the right needle from right to left through the stitch, crossing this needle in front of the left (1). Bring the yarn towards you and then back between the needles (2). Use your right needle to pull the loop through (3) and use it to pull the stitch it came through off the left

cast off

needle (4). Continue for as many purls as you need (5).

You may notice that my knits and purls are exact opposites of each other – they are easy to learn and then play around with when you're more confident. The instructions through this book assume you knit and purl like this, so if it doesn't look like you expect check your technique against mine.

There are two ways to cast off: knitwise and purlwise. Casting off is easy – you simply knit/purl 2 stitches and use your left needle to pull the first over the second and off the needle. You then knit/purl another stitch and pull the previous over that, continuing for as many as you want to cast off. Knitwise will make the casting off chain on the side facing you, purlwise will put the chain on the back.

slip

psso

slip

To slip a stitch simply transfer it from the left needle to the right without working it (1, 2). With yarn in back (wyib) indicates you bring the yarn to the back of the work (if it's not already there) before slipping the stitch, with yarn in front (wyif) means taking the yarn to the front (3, 4). When you've slipped the stitch you'll need to take the yarn back to the side you need it on to continue your row.

psso

psso stands for 'pass the slipped stitch over' and is commonly used to decrease when used with slipped stitches (see Seascape wall hanging pages 112–17). The same method is used for all sorts of things (notably casting off). You use your left needle to hook the second stitch over the first (1) and off (2, 3) from the right needle.

k2tog

p2tog

k2tog

To 'knit 2 together' simply go through 2 stitches instead of one (1), pull the loop through as normal (2, 3) and pull both stitches you went through off together (4).

p2tog

To 'purl 2 together' simply go through 2 stitches instead of one (1), pull the loop through as normal (2, 3) and pull both stitches you went through off together (4).

yo

To make a yarn over (yo) is simple: hold the needles apart with your left hand (1), take the yarn over the right needle (2 – on a purl row bring the yarn back over the needle and towards you between the two) and work the next stitch as normal (3). When you go back across this yo on the following row there are two ways you can work this stitch – with or without a twist. With a twist will close the hole so you have just neatly created a new stitch – when you get to the yo push it forwards (4) and work it as normal (5) according to the stitches before and after it (shown here is a purl row so I've worked it like a purl). When you slip it off the new stitch will have a twist in it.

To create a new stitch and a lace hole work your yo without a twist, and work the yo through the opposite side of the stitch from normal (6, 7). When you slip the new stitch off it will have no twist, creating a hole below it (8).

If you're making a yo between a knit and purl stitch you'll need to work out which method to do to create what you want.

cable

Decide how many stitches wide you want your cable and where it will be in the row. To make your cable slip half its stitches onto a cn (1). Hold this in the front (2) or back of the work (this alters the direction of the cable). Work the second half of the cable (3, 4) then work the first half from the cn (5, 6). This is a complete cable – the standard is to do this once per the same number of rows as the cable is wide in stitches (so 8st wide would be cabled every 8 rows) but you can change this if you want.

When you get the hang of it you can forget the cn – just slide the first half of stitches off (hanging in mid-air on the side of the knitting you want them and keeping your needles close together to avoid dropping these), slip the second half onto the right needle, pick up the first half on the left needle and slip the second half back onto the left too. Then you can work them all in one go. It sounds complicated but it isn't.

The theory of repeats

For the patterns in this book a repeat sequence of stitches in a row is included in (round brackets) or for more complex sequences that require repeats within repeats in [square brackets] and this indicates the section to be repeated. Sometimes a specific number of repeats is required which will be indicated – otherwise just keep going while you have enough stitches to do so.

Buttonholes

Knit indicated number of stitches. Bring the yarn to the front. Slip 1 stitch from the left needle to the right and take the yarn to the back. Drop it there.

Slip another stitch from the left to the right then pass the last slipped stitch over it – a bit like casting off. Keep casting off stitches like this until you have done the correct number for your buttonhole width. Slip the last cast off stitch back to the left needle and turn the piece round so you are facing the other side.

Pick up the yarn you dropped and cast on as many new stitches as you cast off. Then cast on one more but before you put the new stitch on the left needle bring the yarn towards you between the previous stitches and this one.

Turn the work round again.

Slip 1 stitch from the left to the right and pass the last new one over it. Pull your yarn to make sure the buttonhole is firm then continue your row.

Working out stitch tension

Your stitch tension is simply the amount of stitches and rows you personally create per centimetre when using a certain pair of needles and yarn. Yarn companies give

an indication of what you can expect this to be but actually everyone is different. In order to be able to design whatever you want, and use whatever needle/ yarn combination you like, the ability to work this out is super useful!

When you have discovered a particular knit you like you can work out the stitch tension or stitches per centimetre (st/cm) by dividing the number of stitches counted by the number of centimetres covered. For example 10 stitches over 5cm = 2 stitches per cm. Measure your stitches like this in groups – don't ever try to measure individual stitches. To work out the row tension measure a group of rows and do exactly the same calculation. Make sure you follow the same stitch along the rows or it won't be accurate. This sample needs to be about 20 to 30 stitches wide depending on how big the stitches are (more are required for small stitches). Don't measure stitches nearer the edge where the tension will be less consistent. To make this easier put your sample or swatch on a flat surface and use a ruler to squash the piece so you can count the stitches/rows easily at the natural tension without it moving around. Be precise with your measurements – on big pieces especially it does matter.

Then when you decide you want to make something in that stitch/yarn/needle combination simply multiply the width and height by your tension and you'll know how many stitches and rows you need. If your pattern has a repeat you need to check the repeat fits into the number of stitches you need.

Sewing up

The first thing to do is to sew up any seams. To do this place the two pieces you want to sew with their wrong sides together. Use safety pins to hold the pieces together, matching up any points you want to be together. When you cast off you should leave nice long bits of yarn attached to the knitting so you can use these to sew up the seams. Ideally you work from one point to another using a neat overstitch. Make sure you use a nice big, blunt darning needle and go through stitches – do not split the yarn with your stitches. Use the yarn you knitted with to sew, so your stitches will end up invisible.

If your yarn starts to run out do 2 stitches in one place and sew the yarn back down under the stitches you just made. If you need more yarn introduce it by going through these stitches and popping out where you just finished. Always leave about 1–2cm of yarn (depending on the size of the item) sticking out on the inside – when you wash it the end in will felt and shut the seam from unravelling. When you open your piece out, the seam should sit totally flat and the stitches should disappear into the knit.

How to sew up a cushion cover

Take all three pieces of your cover and line them up making sure all your cast-on edges and cast-off edges are in a long line. Also make sure the buttonholes are on the outside edge of the line.

Pin the pieces together (right sides together) and sew down the seams so you have one long piece. Lay this flat, right side up.

Fold the overlap (with buttonhole) so the seam is on the edge and the buttonhole edge is halfway across the front. Pin this together at the top and bottom. Then work out the difference in stitch number between the underlay and overlap, fold the underlay over so the seam is on the edge and it crosses the overlap by this number of stitches. Pin this in place and sew along the top and bottom (through 2 layers on each side and 3 layers in the middle). Turn this the right way out and you'll find you've made an envelope style cover. Put the pad in and sew on the button.

It'll come out in the wash . . .

Knitting can have very different qualities pre- and post-wash – often a bouncy structure can become a wonderful loose drape and vice versa. So, unless you plan on never washing what you're making, it's a good idea to give small knitted samples a wash to see how they will look in the long run rather than assuming they will stay the same. To wash your piece have a look at the instructions on the yarn label. The main things guaranteed to ruin knitting are hot water and a fast, long spin cycle. We always wash our knits in lukewarm water with a mild detergent, rinse them out then put them in to spin on a short slow cycle. We then lie them flat to dry on an airer – not on direct heat. The bigger the piece the more important it is to support the weight as it dries or it can easily distort the shape.

Steam

We are huge fans of steaming – a good steam will transform your wobbly edged cloth into something beautiful. You only need a regular iron with a strong steam setting. Simply put your piece flat on the ironing board in the right shape, then hover the iron over the knitting giving it as much steam as possible. Don't touch the piece with the iron; you only want the steam. Put the iron down and gently pull the piece into shape – as it cools it will set. If you need to you can repeat this until it looks perfect.

Intarsia

Adding contrasting yarns within rows to create vertical contrasting panels is called Intarsia. If your sections start at the cast on you'll need to cast on with the different yarns in their sections. Do the first section

then take the second yarn, tie it to the first close to the needle and cast the next section on (leaving the first yarn where the knot is). When you come to changing from one yarn to another in a row change over as follows; take the first yarn you're using to your left hand and hold it taut, then pick up the second yarn and make your next stitch taking the second over the first you're holding taut. On a purl row do this on the side of the knitting that faces you; on the knit side do it on the back. After a few rows you'll end up with a neat row of stitches where the two yarns join.

If you want to change the width of your stripe, do a trial first to see what happens at the changeover. Big changes will leave you with floats, which some people don't like. They can be sewn in or cut and knotted. You could also add a backing to your piece to hide this.

Cabled footstool sketches

40cm

7cm

30cm

x1

x2

7cm

x2

Side strip

2 x Small Bird Cables

12st Double Cables

3st Basket Stripe

4cm = **8st**

3.7cm = **12st**

1cm = **3st**

+ 1 edge stitch = cast on 24st

Top

4st cable

4st cable

Basket stitch

Apple Pie stitch

Basket stitch

8cm = **24st**

1.3cm = **4st**

18.4cm = **61st**

1.3cm = **4st**

8cm = **24st**

+ 6 single stitches between each pattern = cast on 126st

Side strip length

Cable has row repeat = 3.3row/cm

= 40cm sections

20cm = 66rows = 4 repeats approx each half

15cm = 50rows = 3 repeats each half

WRITING PATTERNS

To write your own pattern you first need to do some sketches to work out the design you want. Then measure your object in panels and write down the size of each one.

You'll need to do some samples of the stitches you want using the yarn and needle size you'll use for the project. Use these to work out the stitch tension and apply this to each part of each panel, which will show you the stitches and rows required. To write the pattern for each panel see Combining Different Stitch Patterns on page 142. You can see in this sketch how I have worked out each section and the full pattern is on page 94–97, where you can also see the finished article.

Combining different stitch patterns

Do a sketch of what you'd like to make – you can play around with your samples to see how the patterns look together. Start with something with a simple shape, such as a cushion or a throw and then decide the size. Start to work out what area you would like to cover with each pattern across the width. Think about whether you would like some kind of detail on the edge, and include this in your working out. When you know your measurements across the width you can use these to work out how many stitches each section of pattern will need (be careful to make sure any repeats work out with this number). Then add all the stitches required together – this is your cast on number.

To work out the rows, you need to work out an average between the tensions of the different patterns. If the row tensions are similar this will even them out just fine for your calculations. Multiply your desired length by this tension and that is how many rows you need.

Be aware that if you have two patterns with vastly different row tensions as vertical stripes, the one with more rows per cm will start to create gathers in the one with less. Try not to do this to start with. (Later on though you can try this intentionally – when exploited this looks really pretty.)

When you write your pattern you need all your instructions for each row of each pattern – work across each row applying the relevant pattern to the number of stitches required. Don't forget that your drawing is seen from the right side so the written pattern will follow the different sections in order from right to left. On the back of the fabric you need to follow the pattern layout in your drawing from left to right.

Knitting Circles

Total circumference = Xcm

Radius in cm by row tension = ?r

Total circumference x cm / number of sections = Ycm. Cast Cast on per section = Ycm multiplied by stitch tension = ?st

To deal with circles is surprisingly easy and this method will help you work out the pattern for either 2 needles (a seam will be required) or for 4 needles. Measure the circle's circumference and radius. You knit your circle from the outside in, so you can use these measurements to work out how many and how often you decrease your stitches to get to zero in the centre.

If you cast on the circumference then decrease stitches off each side you end up with a triangle, so think of your circle as cake with slices. By dividing it and then decreasing a little bit in each section you will end up with a shape that is circular.

For 8 sections you work your pattern out like this:

1 Divide your circumference in cm by the number of sections (80cm circumference / 8 = 10cm per section).

2 Multiply the section width by the stitch tension (1st/cm x 10 = 10st per section).

3 Take your radius measurement and multiply it by your row tension (10cm radius x 2r/cm = 20 rows).

4 Now you know that between the outside of the circle and the centre you have to get rid of 10st over 20 rows. To find out how often you decrease divide the rows by stitches (20rows / 10st = 1st per 2 rows).

5 To cast on, multiply the stitches for each section by the number of sections in your circle (10st x 8 sections = 80st cast on) and repeat your instructions for each sections row 8 times to work across the whole piece (Row 1 'k8 k2tog' x 8).

6 You'll need to use your judgement as to how to lose the last few stitches; just try it out to see what works.

Converting shaped drawings to instructions

The first thing that often surprises non-knitters is that you don't need a paper pattern to work from – what you do need is a good set of measurements.

Basically you need to know how wide you want your piece to start off and then how much you need to decrease or increase, and where, over a certain distance. You convert all these measurements to stitches (all widths) and rows (all lengths).

To deal with curves you do really need to draw them as the actual size. Then you use a ruler and make your curve into a series of straight lines. Try to make it into as few as possible and then work out the width and height of each line to find out what stitches/rows are required and how much you add/take away per row.

Curves

?cm=?st

?cm=?r

?cm=?r

?cm=?r

increasing section +?st/?r

—————— line of curve required

- - - - - - lines drawn to make curve into series of straight lines

decreasing section -?st/?r

direction of knit

direction of knit

?cm=?st

?cm=?r

?cm=?st

?cm=?st

Make sure your sections, rows and stitches are measured at a right angle to the direction of the knitting, which is shown to the left of the curved line.

suppliers

SOURCES FOR YARNS USED IN THIS BOOK
www.debbieblissonline.com
www.knitrowan.com
www.patonsyarns.com

SOURCES FOR RIBBON USED IN THIS BOOK
www.texere-yarns.co.uk

acknowledgements

I would like to thank every one involved in making this book happen:
My lovely, patient and determined knitters who helped knit the samples –
thank you so much Brenda Watson, Ann McFaull, Brenda Jennings,
Joan Doyle, Pauline Dodd, Doreen Payne, Sally Cuthbert and Brenda Willows

Sophie for her endless sewing and organizing skills

Debbie Bliss for her lovely yarn

I would also like to thank all my family who are endlessly supportive no
matter how much knitting there is about the place!

All photography is by Ben Anders, apart from the image on pages 8 to 9, which is by Polly Eltes,
and the images far left on page 131 and left on page 138, which are by Ruth Cross.